T0167030

# Help Me Live ... As I Die

## Cancer vs.
## the Power of Love

## Joe Peterson

iUniverse, Inc.
Bloomington

# Help Me Live ... As I Die
## Cancer vs. the Power of Love

*iUniverse books may be ordered through booksellers or by contacting:*

*iUniverse*
*1663 Liberty Drive*
*Bloomington, IN 47403*
*www.iuniverse.com*
*1-800-Authors (1-800-288-4677)*

*ISBN: 978-1-475-94095-4 (pbk)*
*ISBN: 978-1-475-94096-1 (cloth)*
*ISBN: 978-1-475-94097-8 (ebk)*
*Library of Congress Control Number: 2012913914*

*Printed in the United States of America*

*iUniverse rev. date: 9/12/2012*

# Contents

# Introduction

On February 21, 1998, I traveled with a group of friends from St. Paul to Duluth, Minnesota, for a weekend getaway. Our first night out drinking and socializing, we gathered around a table. We were at one of the gay bars in the Northland area, and I was disappointed because none of the patrons were my type, when suddenly a very good-looking guy popped his head between two friends sitting across from me. The first thing that grabbed my attention: his pearly whites; he had a beautiful smile. The second thing I noticed: his pretty green eyes; they really seemed to be a gateway to his soul. He emitted confidence, and his aura felt visible to my eyes; he was so vibrant. He introduced himself. "Hi, I'm Kelly. Where are you guys from?" We chatted a little but never exchanged numbers.

On March 6, 1998, my best friend and I attended my cousin's wedding in Duluth. Our entire drive from St. Paul consisted of me talking about Kelly and hoping I would get an opportunity to see him again. I was smitten. After the wedding reception, we went to a different gay bar, sat with our drinks, and waited. Through the open door walked Kelly and a friend. I was excited but extremely nervous to converse with him. There was definitely a nonverbal acknowledgment we were attracted to one another. Kelly loved to dance, and when he took the floor, I was mesmerized. Kel would move his upper body in a flowing side-to-side movement and stroke his chin with his right hand.

His facial expressions were a playful flirtation with life. I knew he had hit his groove when, one by one, he would raise each leg off the ground and do a step-by-step slither while remaining in the same place. Put it all together and I was hooked. I have always been self-conscious about my dancing abilities, but Kel cut loose at the edge of the dance floor for all to see. Confident and comfortable, he was having fun and was oblivious anyone was around—unless they could add to the party.

Before I headed back to St. Paul, we went for breakfast and exchanged information. Kelly was from Cloquet, Minnesota, a small town twenty minutes south of Duluth and one hour and forty-five minutes from my home. It took me three times to say his last name, Boedigheimer, correctly. He worked for Black Bear Casino in Carlton and was a dedicated employee. We made plans to talk on the phone, and neither of us could have predicted it would blossom into a thirteen-and-a-half year relationship. At least three weekends per month, during the first year-and-a half, we took turns traveling to see one another. It was a preview of living and growing together. After a few months, we were introduced to each other's families. I am the youngest of twelve and wasn't quite sure how Kelly would adapt to my large family, but he was immediately accepted and loved. Surprisingly, his family of six (including his mom and dad) was much louder than mine. Over the thirteen years, our families bonded, and though we weren't legally able to wed, they viewed us as married.

Our first New Year's together, Kelly took me on my first out-of-state vacation by plane—one of many vacations to come. We tried to make every destination one of sun and warmth, because the hotter the weather, the richer the tan. This also

January 1999

November 2009

meant frequent tanning-bed sessions, preparing our bodies for the real deal. We never wore sunscreen, and many times Kelly would get overexposed, but any reddening would always turn tan. During one beach-driven vacation, a man approached Kelly and told him to cover his head because it was burned. Within a few days, Kel was able to lift a dead layer of skin from his scalp. With a hat on for protection, we were soon back on the beach. We loved our vacations, and we loved our time together. Now they're just a memory.

Our cancer journey began in August of 2010: Kelly had an ingrown hair on his chin. He was prone to getting them and went about this one his usual way: popping, squeezing, prodding, and poking. After a few weeks, Kel went to extremes. He used a razor blade and sliced into this blueberry-sized bump and extracted what looked like tiny clear balls. The pressure was released, but the problem persisted.

Reluctantly and without having a family physician, Kel finally made a doctor's appointment. Even though he had insurance, he hated the idea of paying a deductible, which was part of the reason why he postponed having his chin looked at. During the first appointment, the doctor cut into Kel's bump and dug the culprit out: the ingrown hair that had caused him grief. As soon as it was removed, the specimen was shown to Kelly, and then he was bandaged and released.

Within a few days, Kel found himself back at his doctor's. The bump had grown back, larger this time. The doctor sliced into it, cutting and removing scar tissue before cauterizing the entire area. Kel's wound was internally packed with gauze, and he was told to let it heal from the inside out. The gauze was evicted by his body's will, and Kelly had to repack the wound, but the location of it proved to be difficult to maintain. In order to keep the gauze in the wound, bandaging was wrapped around his head to keep constant pressure on the area. Needless to say, Kel hated the entire contraption, but we both did the best we could to fulfill the requirements. The tissue removals were sent to the lab and tested. Nothing out of the ordinary was discovered.

The positive results from the second procedure lasted a couple of weeks. Kel enjoyed a few days without bandages and a flat surface on the right side of his chin. Unfortunately, these joys were followed by another bump that eventually surpassed the size of the last. We were told that cells can mutate quickly (for whatever reason) and they would have to be a bit more aggressive with the next removal. A plastic surgeon performed the third procedure and confirmed he was aggressive with the

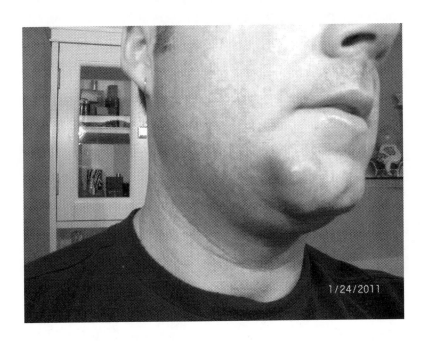

1/24/2011

tissue removal, but he did not feel comfortable taking any more than he did. Within three days, another lump began to grow.

Kelly scheduled an appointment to discuss the mass regrowth and was under the impression that this visit would consist only of scheduling another surgery. Kel asked if he should have another person accompany him but was assured driving wouldn't be an issue and it was unnecessary to have anyone along. I offered to drive him, but Kel believed it was just a follow-up. During this visit, Kelly learned he had melanoma.

Kel told me the doctor came in, introduced the assisting nurse, and stated her purpose was to observe and learn. Kelly wondered if that was her true purpose. After he was told of his melanoma status, Kel was in shock but held it together because he didn't want to cry in front of them. The doctor left the room, and the nurse sat with Kel until he received a cancer consult recommendation. Kelly's cancer journey began without the support of a loved one. There was no undoing the damage that was possibly done to his psyche. He was set free to drive home alone with his thoughts. Kelly was a private individual; showing emotion wasn't comfortable for him, even in private, but he was crying when he called me. I immediately headed home.

We met with the cancer consultant together. After sharing her limited knowledge regarding melanoma, she touched Kel's face and said, "Oh, honey, they will have to remove your jaw." As she made that statement, her pager went off and she rushed out the door. While Kel sobbed, I tried to stay composed, but we both sat in disbelief and fear. When the consultant returned, she neglected to comment further on her previous remark, and I had to redirect her. She then admitted she wasn't well versed in melanoma and she wanted us to seek professional care outside of Duluth. She phoned a friend at the Mayo Clinic and made Kelly's appointment. We left fearing Kel would lose his jaw.

On February 5, 2011, I created Kelly's Caring Bridge site and kept our loved ones updated and informed. His CB journey began with me writing a background story, which concluded with "Kel is in good spirits, and we are absorbing all of your positive energy and thoughts. Love to you all."

# Chapter One

## The Beginning Battle

### Monday, February 7, 2011

The night before, Kelly and I celebrated because we were anxious to begin this journey yet nervous about the unknown. We drove to the Mayo Clinic in Rochester, Minnesota, and prepared ourselves for the following day's appointments.

We met with several doctors, and they confirmed it was melanoma but Kelly would not lose his jaw. They felt a large removal of skin near his jaw, outside and inside, was the best treatment. Because of the severity of the trouble melanoma can wreak, the doctors found it necessary to remove more tissue, which allowed less chance of leaving behind any of the cancer. They told us they would try to stretch the skin on his face to cover the hole left from the removal. If they were unable to achieve satisfactory results, they would remove skin from his inner left arm, which was the closest skin match, to patch the area. We knew Kel's face would be altered, but we believed he wouldn't be changed.

2/6/2011

**On February 6, Kelly asked me to take his picture with his parents. This photo (along with a few others) accompanied him during every trip throughout 2011.**

Kelly had three scans—CT, MRI, and PET—and each came back negative, which meant the cancer had not spread elsewhere. Kelly hadn't been told what stage the cancer had reached, but we hoped his surgery scheduled for Thursday would be the only necessary treatment. Kel was told he would be out of work for six weeks, and his full recovery could take up to one year.

I was feeling confident and secure about Kel's life, but the terror, fear, and wondering had set in for Kel. It was really difficult knowing his heavy burden hadn't really been lifted. He had new realities weighing on him. I believed Kel would be as good as new and even better because of this experience. I also felt Kelly and I would become closer. It became my responsibility to encourage and support him as we both became enlightened by life's experiences.

## Tuesday, February 8, 2011

Even though we got home late the night before, Kelly went into work. He was dedicated and wanted to make sure he wasn't leaving anyone with potential problems or unresolved issues. His focus on getting healthy began after everyone's needs were met. When I called him, he was very positive and upbeat; his fears seemed minimal. I felt his confidence through his positivity. He took control and sought regularity.

## February 9 and 10, 2011

We drove back to Rochester Wednesday evening and spent quality time together. Both of us were anxious for surgery to be over, but Kel was also very nervous.

Thursday morning, Kelly's spirits were high as we walked to the surgery check-in desk. After we checked in, the prep nurse referred to Kel's surgeons as the "dream team." She admitted that she got goose bumps from their achievements. How could we not feel blessed? I felt ecstatic and was confident Kelly was sharing my optimism. Throughout the morning, we laughed and made light of everything around us. Others responded and reacted to our joy and laughter, and we realized again that life is to be celebrated. Before the nurse wheeled him out for surgery, she checked his blood pressure and pulse. They were at resting numbers. Kel was in the moment and obviously comfortable in their care. We, as a whole, were a team.

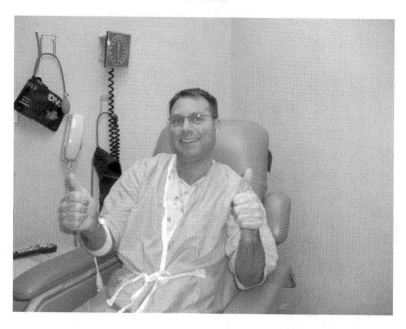

The first incision was made at 9:11 a.m., and I believed Kel was very much aware of all the positive energy being sent to him. By 1:15 p.m., I received the second update. He was doing very well. They were prepping the neck region and getting ready to remove the flap. The flap, tissue taken from Kel's left inner forearm, was used in rebuilding his facial area. I was grateful for the physical support from our families because my mental state was slowly weakening as I visualized the surgical process. Another update at 3:45 p.m.: surgeons were establishing circulation in his arm. A major artery was removed with the flap to ensure an adequate source for blood flow. Tendons, muscles, and veins were exposed after the flap removal, and a graft from the top of his left thigh was stitched over the area. The major artery for the flap still needed to be attached to another blood source in his facial/neck region. Finally, at 4:50 p.m., I was told they were closing him up.

We had many reasons to celebrate after surgery. Only a small part of Kel's inner cheek had to be removed with the mass, so surgeons were able to close the inside of his mouth using surrounding flesh. All of the lymph nodes were negative. The main facial vein was unaffected by melanoma; therefore, Kelly's muscles would be weak but able to regain their functionality. Kel planned on wearing the battle scars with pride, and I was proud of him.

Kel's mom, sisters, and I waited in the hall as the staff rolled him to his room. I said, "Hey, Bucko, how are you?" His eyes opened so wide I thought I scared the shit out of him.

He said, "Hi," which was drawn out and sounded more like "Hiiiiiiiiii." He shut his eyes and then opened them again, looked at me, and sarcastically said, "Nice shirt!" It read, "Everything Alters Me, but Nothing Changes Me," and every time I wore it, he'd whine and ask me to change. There was a rich meaning within the words, but Kel liked fun clothes and he thought this T-shirt was dull. I had always found strength in the words, and during this cancer reality, he was slowly finding a soft spot for the words as well. He proved he still had a sense of humor and knew I wore the shirt just for him.

I wasn't prepared for what I saw when they rolled him by. Kelly was not bandaged, and I was fearful for what his own reaction would be when he saw himself. The skin from Kel's arm was stitched onto his face in a two-by-two-inch square. The color match was close, but the lack of facial hair threw me a little. His face was very swollen, and tubes seemed to be coming and going everywhere. The bandages he did have were blood-soaked, and he was in pain. The best part of all: when I looked at him, his eyes pierced my heart just like always! Altered but not changed.

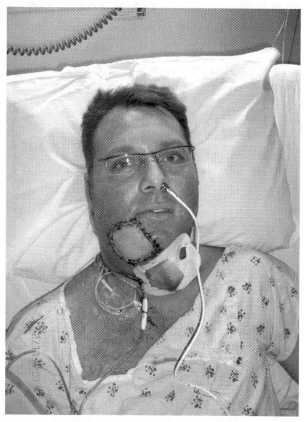

**The morning after surgery.**

## Friday, February 11, 2011

Doctors visited Kelly in the morning and repeated that all the lymph nodes had come back negative. From what we had learned from previous appointments, surgery was the only procedure needed, and we were ecstatic it was over.

Before visiting Kel, his family and I sat in our hotel lobby, making a pact to avoid discussions of his appearance. Before seeing any visitors, Kel used his bathroom and caught a glimpse of himself in the mirror. Though it was a brief peek, he shared his initial thoughts with us: "Great, I look like a freak show. I look like I've got my ass on my face." We were relieved his humor was intact and he was doing excellent: aware and alert. It was amazing how much the swelling had gone down in a matter of hours, and I began to investigate his surgical sites. Kelly got annoyed with me and told every visitor that his mom and I were poking around and checking things out. While waving his uncast arm in the air, abruptly and loudly, he said, "I'm gonna start charging dollars! Get your peek for dollars!" He even told me to shut up so he could try to sleep. I never felt so happy to hear his sarcasm; I loved it. Kel was constantly watching everyone's eyes. As people stared upon him, he attempted to interpret the stories their eyes told.

Kelly's right arm had been throbbing all day, so an ultrasound was done to rule out blood clots. It appeared to be a muscle cramp caused from surgery. His left arm looked like a wiffle bat; the cast thickness was massive. Kelly had difficulty raising this arm because of the weight. Thankfully, it would be removed in five days. He had some minor pain during the day, but it wasn't until evening that it really reared its ugly head. I was unaware if Kel thought he needed to endure as much pain as possible, but it was obviously difficult for him to request more meds or clearly define his pain level. It was imperative for his personal comfort that Kelly learn to guide and inform the staff of his needs.

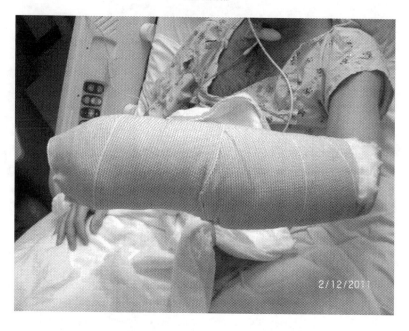

Though several tubes were already removed, he still had the feeding tube running up his nose and into his stomach. We were told that if everything continued to heal properly, it would be removed before his discharge. The nurses warned that his leg skin graft would cause much pain, but Kel was walking with little discomfort. After telling Kelly how great he looked, the night nurse proceeded to give us examples of what she had seen after this type of surgery. She painted some monstrous images, and we felt fortunate to have gotten the dream team.

No one wanted to leave Kel's side, and I feared that he would have too much alone time and spiral into sadness. It was difficult seeing him sad, hurt, or crying. I had witnessed these emotions plenty of times over the past weeks. I also knew I needed to let him go through his own process, and, in doing so, he would become stronger. We had a good talk, and we were going to get through this together.

## Saturday, February 12, 2011

Kelly finally slept; unfortunately it was achieved in two-hour intervals. He told me he was feeling much better, and I was sure it was due to rest. Though he was getting tired of hearing it, Kelly was looking great. His facial swelling had greatly reduced, and the flap had flattened out around the edges and begun meshing with the surrounding areas. The flap looked like a square piece of fabric hemmed on all sides and stitched onto another piece of fabric. Just one day earlier, it could have been picked by a fingernail as if it were a separate piece of skin, but the flap was now becoming part of his face. With Kel's permission, I began taking daily pictures so the healing improvements would be captured. If we ever doubted progress, proof would be available.

If going home had been based on mobility, Kel would have been released, but he was required to stay until the gadget in his neck was removed. It was embedded near the flap and echoed the sound of blood flow. As long as we could hear it, the flap was functioning properly. If the blood flow stopped, surgeons would have to act immediately in order to save the tissue. There were so many scary scenarios, but Kel's body was accepting everything the way we had hoped.

It was completely amazing witnessing how Kel's body healed, and the only impact was on his attitude and how he treated himself mentally, physically, and verbally. As we embraced

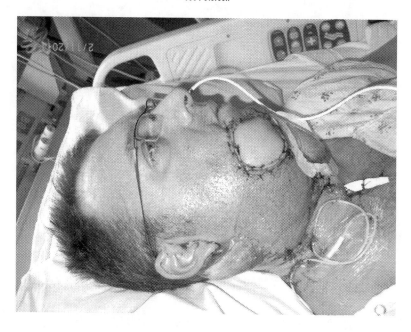

the circumstances, we attained confidence, strength, and knowledge. We weren't perfect—just human.

## Sunday, February 13, 2011

"Really good," Kel described his present state. Throughout the night, his pain was horrible, but he felt much better after they removed his feeding tube. Before removing his leg bandage, nurses drained the bodily fluids that had pooled underneath. Three extra large syringes extracted the deep red mass. The bandage was removed, and a fresh see-through one was applied over the graft. I took pictures and checked things out, to which Kel said, "Okay, you're close enough!"

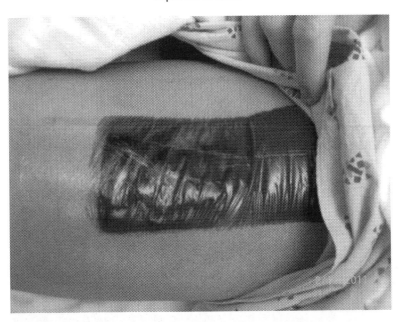

Kelly took a big step this day: the mirror. I wanted him to see what had been happening, to witness what my eyes were seeing. I listened as he said, "Eh, I thought it was all the way back to my ear because it hurt so bad. Oh my God is my face fat." He chuckled. "Eh, I can't believe how swollen I am." There was a long pause. "*Uuuuuuug-ly!* Okay I'm done. That's enough for today." It was less emotional than what I'd prepared for, and (I think) not as bad as what Kel had imagined. The pain he had experienced made him assume the flap had covered an area from his chin to his ear, but it was actually caused by the lymph node removals.

We learned Kel had a rare type of melanoma. It was deep, large, concentrated, and fast-growing. Knowledge about this type was limited because it was isolated to one area, so his case was documented to assist in future education and teaching. We also found out a total of fifty-five lymph nodes were removed during his surgery, and doctors were baffled because each was negative. Because Kel's was such a rare, special case, radiation was advised.

Despite all of the positive successes, Kel had a battle within that no one could understand or relate to. He was having a difficult time and stated he just wanted to wake up from the nightmare. I wanted him to continue sharing what he was feeling and thinking. There was a fear of the unknown, but I believed knowledge would help us grow and move forward. As the day progressed, so did his pain. Before heading to my parents' home, I tried to leave him with happy thoughts and, I hoped, a healthier state of mind. I reminded him of the support within reach and kissed him before I left. My gut told me even after he was physically healed, the emotional healing was going to take more time. I had every belief both would connect and forever bring the value of his true self to light.

## Monday, February 14, 2011

It was a rocky night of sleep. The pain was minimal, but Kel's discomfort was not. He slept in but was woken by one of his doctors. The drainage tube was removed from his chin; we couldn't wait until all the tubes were out. Anything and everything acted as a basin for the drainage tubes. They dribbled and dripped everywhere.

Getting up close and personal (again), I realized the incision started at the top right inner ear, where it met his cheek bone, continued one inch above shoulder level, and came up the middle of his chin, where it met the flap. After surgery, Kel was so swollen I couldn't see the incision the way I was seeing it this day. Fifty-five nodes were removed during the procedure, and my stomach churned at the thought. I ended up with nervous giggles. I had been there too long and the reality was starting to get to me.

Kel had a very good day, and we shared several walks in the hospital halls. His pain was as stable as his mood, and we were anxious to get him home. We bickered for the first time in a very long time, and it felt good. I wasn't going to be easy on him during recovery. Just like every discussion, I was expecting him to argue every point. I was excited for our first bickerfest (verbal banter consisting of arguing, fighting, yelling, understanding, and play) and the acknowledgment that followed: our relationship was solid. A big sigh of relief accompanied that thought.

We read Kelly's Caring Bridge site and were emotional. Reading the journal and guestbook supplied us with strength and confidence that had not yet been tapped into. It was strange for me to read along with him because I wrote the updates and now I was going to pay the consequences if he hated my entries. He got teary at some, laughed at others, and rolled his eyes at many. Ultimately, Caring Bridge was a uniting and strengthening resource, feeding the universal energy force meant for Kelly.

## Tuesday, February 15, 2011

Hospital smells were making my stomach weak, and the atmosphere was draining. Thank God Kel was getting discharged. It was *Kelly Unplugged*, and we were definitely fans. The remaining drainage tubes were removed, and the cast was replaced with a splint. He was released, and we headed home. During our drive, we received a call from the Mayo Clinic informing us Kelly would be needing radiation. An appointment was scheduled, and within a week we'd have to return to Rochester. I was so focused on Kel's recovery that the news of radiation and more procedures knocked the wind out of my sails. No matter what Kel had to endure, I would be with him.

The ride home was torturous for Kel. Every bump, crack, and pothole caused painful awareness at each surgical site. We stopped at my parents' home in St. Paul to visit, rest, and get Chaos, our eight-year-old Bichon. Though he missed his little guy, Kel feared his loving hyperactivity. After using the bathroom, Kel rejoined the group and said, "Damn, those lights in the bathroom are bright. I'm not used to seeing everything in the mirror so clearly. I look like I'm storing nuts for the winter." His humor made us laugh and offered comfort.

We began the final two-hour drive home, and Chaos was quarantined to the backseat. Oddly enough, he was bugging me the entire ride. He was stretching his body from the backseat and laying his head on either of my shoulders so I could pet him. Every once in a while, he would go near Kel with his fluttering nostrils, and then he'd retreat. Kel was still oozing from areas where the tubes were, and obviously that odor repulsed Chaos. I felt bad for my boys because I knew how much they loved each other, but their affection was limited. It was a very confusing time.

I wanted to erase this nightmare, if even for five minutes, but I knew we didn't have time to waste on such impossible desires. Every aspect of life had been altered, and Kelly was no longer in a safe zone: the hospital. Challenges waited as he reentered the world, and I became increasingly aware that I had been taking simple things for granted. It may have felt like we were in a never-ending nightmare, but sharing our lives was a dream.

**Six days after surgery, Kelly and Chaos reunite.**

# Chapter Two

## *Home*

### Tuesday, February 15, 2011

If anyone thought Kelly looked rough, I was prepared to verbally defend him and educate the person. Imagine how anyone would look after having part of his face cut out and patched with part of his arm. He also had the leg graft, bruises on his right arm from all of the needle stabs, an incision from ear to chin, and an oozing rash on his back. Considering the circumstances, Kelly looked amazing, and we needed to be surrounded by positive, understanding forces. He was going through something I could only try to comfort and support. When Kelly was angry and directed it my way, I accepted it as best I could.

Even though Kel was at one of the best facilities in the country, many improvements were needed. I had witnessed a few indiscretions, and during the drive home, Kel filled me in on more. When Kelly was admitted into the hospital, he had a preexisting mild rash on his back. During the weekend of his

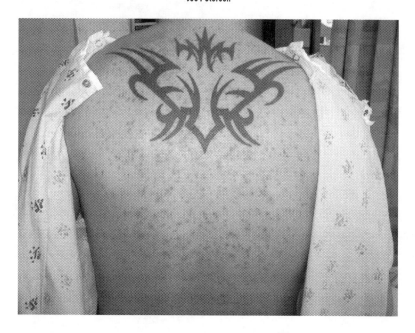

stay, many areas had oozed and dried to the sheets. Only after he voiced his concern did they begin using hypoallergenic sheets. Only once did nurses apply lotion to his back.

Each day of the weekend, I noticed dried blood on Kelly's chest from the drainage tube. Kel informed me the weekend staff had neglected to clean him, and I had to request action in order to get results. Bandages were bloodied and falling from their proper locations. I had to ask for their replacements. Exercise was not encouraged or guided during the weekend, and Kel was left to motivate and fend for himself. When we arrived home, I washed Kel's back. Several areas bled and were so painful he winced as I touched them. After reevaluating these occurrences, it was decided that I would monitor and enforce Kel's quality of care. Up to this point, Kel and I did the best we could, but we felt some professionals let us down. Even if he got demanding and bitchy, I felt his home care would be the best. The biggest difference between the hospital staff and me was that Kel would have to deal with my overbearing, loving involvement.

Kelly rested on his usual couch, and Chaos growled because he wanted to lie with his daddy like always. Unfortunately, Kel was too sore and couldn't risk four legs and a wild tongue being near him. It looked like I would be nurturing both of them for a while. Kel slept for numerous hours, and it was a great beginning of familiarity—home, the place where Kelly's healing could really begin. It was an opportunity to replace emotional overload with feelings of self-worth and daily appreciation.

## Wednesday, February 16, 2011

I took time to read over paperwork from Kel's surgery. A 7 by 10 cm area was removed from his face. The melanoma mass was 2.2 by 2.0 by 1.6 cm, and they removed surrounding tissue in case the cancer had spread. The forearm flap dimensions were 5 by 11 cm, and the skin was doubled over upon itself to get the right thickness to fill and patch Kel's face. The blood vessels from the flap were brought into the neck region to assure proper blood flow. The leg skin graft was 7 by 16 cm. I had a better understanding of Kel's physical pain, and I knew we both had mental challenges ahead.

If February 16 were titled, it would have been called *Emotional Presence*. Lying on the couch, Kel circled his face with his hand and said, "I feel like I was shot in the head." Kelly was accustomed to an active lifestyle, and he was now in a state of need. He cried and apologized because he felt guilty that I had several new responsibilities placed upon me. I tried to assure him there was no other place I'd rather be, but I could see he felt like a burden. I witnessed more tears in two weeks than in the previous thirteen years we had shared together. I knew there were things Kel wished I wouldn't include in my Caring Bridge updates, but I felt true, honest feelings could never be used against someone. I soon realized Kel was not an emotional open book like me and his outpourings seemed to embarrass him. I shared my thoughts regarding internalized emotions; I felt they could turn against and potentially harm one's body. I wanted him to feel safe when he cried and flush away some baggage from within. I was proud of our emotions; if we felt like crying, we should have been proud every time we did so.

I had yet to ask why this was happening to Kelly, but questioned if he had been. His response was "I haven't asked why. I just figured it was karma."

I asked, "Karma, for what?" He didn't really have an answer. "Why?" may not have been a question Kel had, but he had some sort of belief that he did or didn't do something and karma had come to wreak havoc. I was certain his answer would be different moment by moment, yet it proved that internal struggles and questions continued. I wasn't sure if I believed in karma of this magnitude, and even if I did, I couldn't fathom anything Kel had done in his life that would be punishable by cancer.

His personal energy needed to be put to better use, like healing and acceptance. This was a part of the equation we would work on together.

Kel mentioned he didn't feel worthy of the support being put forth, but I hoped he'd discover a way to allow every act of love into his life and absorb all of the positivity sent his way. Kel was very private, but he became less so as I shared our journey on Caring Bridge. I knew he may have an issue with some of my writings, but their sole purpose was building a source of positive energy. Cancer brought dynamic changes, and Kelly took the opportunity to develop and refine every aspect of his life. The surface was once his focus, but he began to step inside his core, searching for insight and peace. Cancer was educating us, and somehow we had to trust our lives were going to be enriched even though it was presently perceived as devastation.

We had been together thirteen years, a long time for any relationship but a rarity in the gay community. Kel and I were frequently asked, "How have you made it work? What's your secret?" We were always perplexed by the questions because our shared lives felt natural. We were having fun, but more importantly, we were always allowing personal growth and learning from one another. Even if there was physical distance between us, we remained emotionally connected. We loved being together and near one another, and we slept peacefully at night.

## Thursday, February 17, 2011

"Oh, what a beautiful morning. Oh, what a beautiful day!" Kel was feeling awesome and I was feeling gay.

The previous night before bed, Chaos had scaled the back of the couch Kel rested on. Finally, he was able to give his daddy a kiss as Kelly invited him to squeeze between him and the couch back. It was a special happy reunion, and Chaos continued to give kisses for several minutes. They snuggled and crashed until Chaos left his side at 10:30 a.m. It was therapeutic healing time for both of them.

The morning of surgery was the last time Kel was able to wash his hair. It wasn't difficult imagining how great it felt to wash again, because he was verbally expressing his ecstasy while I shampooed it. After showering, he reminded me of a pregnant woman: a glowing smile from ear to ear. Kel was revitalized, smelling and looking better. After we swabbed his stitched areas, Kel acknowledged how much the swelling had gone down. He was painfully aware of one area behind his right ear. With a three-way mirror, he viewed the hole left from the drainage tube's removal. I had a tough stomach, but I got the nervous giggles every time I cleaned around this area. The tube left a triangular opening measuring two- to three-eighths of an inch on every side. Every time Kel moved his head, the secretions within moved up and down, like a clogged drain. My giggles started, and I explained to Kel I was afraid my swabbing Q-tip would get lodged in there. Because there was drainage, Kel kept his head upright 24/7. Towels were wrapped loosely around his neck so drippings were contained. We made a good team and won every challenge.

When I stared at Kelly, seeing only the left side of his face, it felt like just another day. I found reassurance wherever I could, and Kel was finding his. After he shared his feelings, I was brought to tears. With his swollen face, pained experiences, and muttered speech, Kel looked at me and said, "Want a pill?" We busted up laughing and knew there was more laughter ahead.

Before company arrived, we straightened up and Kel said, "Let's light a candle. Let's keep it normal." This simple action could have gone without a second thought, but Kel's behavior was proof we were moving forward. Adapting to change was part of our survival instincts, and Kel's were in motion. I was there to propel them if they faltered. Our beautiful morning shined throughout the day. We were blessed and grateful.

## Friday, February 18, 2011

*Guess who? No, it's not Joe ... it is me, Kelly.*

*Where to start? The past couple of weeks have flown by in warp speed, except for moments when I lay in bed and think about everything. Reading your posts has done something for me that can't be expressed in words. As you have read, it has been very emotional; however, most of the emotions haven't been because of the alterations to my face but because of the love and support I have felt throughout this whole journey. In the future, when I look at my face it is going to mean something different to me. It's going to be for the better—it is making me a better person. I'm realizing not to take little things, and definitely not others, for granted. I feel good, my head hurts, and I am so overwhelmed by everyone's love. I also look forward to seeing all of you and being able to put this behind me with a smile.*

*Sincerely feeling your love and kind words!*

*Kelly*

## Saturday, February 19, 2011

Kel fixed his hair. He was feeling very good and it was awesome to witness the return of a normal routine. Seeing him so polished was extremely gratifying for me and a boost to his esteem. First-time visitors' comments were positive reinforcements of the healing progress. Kel admitted he was happy I had been taking daily pictures because it helped him push through discouraging moments. Seeing is believing, and he was shown proof every day.

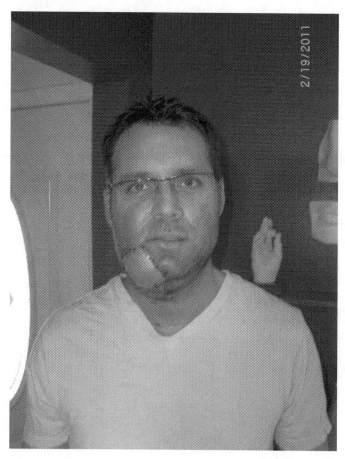

Kel used a beard trimmer to get rid of some of his facial hair, and in doing so, less emphasis was placed on the flap. Some mistook it for a bandage. Witnessing day-to-day healing progress was amazing, but replacing bandages was gross! The covering on his leg was like plastic wrap, and it stuck to every area except the wound. That particular bandage was meant to keep all fluids in, but as more secretions pooled, the adhesion weakened. We either had to replace it or let it leak. Neither choice was pleasant. As I peeled back the bandage, the flood gates opened and the blood-red pool flowed onto my hand and floor. I was not prepared! I got bloody once. Kel would have to change it next time. Drippings from the drainage holes had slowed and Kelly was free from towel scarves. I heard and read about the procedure done on Kelly's arm, but they didn't paint the results I saw. The rectangular skin graft, taken from his leg, was stitched onto his inner arm. At the top of the graft, an incision surpassed the bend of his inner arm and stopped shy of his bicep. The entire site looked like a giant square sperm, but grayish in color. The stitching detail bordering the graft was large and intricate, while the thin barrier of skin protected his tendons and muscles. If there was a sight for sore eyes, it was his back rash. It was so much better, but it was difficult to stop Kel's scratching.

Forget baby steps, we were striving for huge leaps. Everything was stabilizing, and we were content with the reality. We stayed home the entire weekend. It was out of our ordinary and yet it was oddly peaceful, fun, and cheap. I could have assumed it was our new normal, but our routine was being redefined every day as we battled back and achieved the results we wanted.

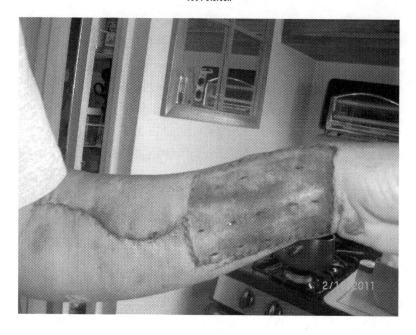

## Sunday, February 20, 2011

The day after company became a day of rest and recovery. Kel may have put forth more energy for our guests than he should have, but he was feeling good and took advantage of the opportunity. Inside was peaceful, quiet, and uneventful, but outside was a mighty wind storm. We drove to Lake Superior and witnessed the waves rolling and crashing as Mother Nature was wreaking havoc. I couldn't help but think that regardless of that storm's destruction, life would continue. We have the choice to live every moment or let it pull us under as we drown.

On our way home, Kelly made his first in-town shopping appearance. As we walked the aisles, one hand held his scarf over his chin, covering any operative evidence. I tried to boost his confidence, reminding him to wear every scar, stitch, and detail with pride. It was a good, uneventful experience yet, unfortunately, Kel was self-consciously aware of every step he walked. No matter; this was an achievement, and I was proud he walked with me.

After Kelly agreed to try sleeping in our bed, we gathered all the pillows and pried him off the couch. I was usually a pillow hoarder (and he used to complain about it), but he had six-plus pillows on his side in order to keep him upright and comfy. Chaos was maneuvering, trying to find a nice warm spot in between his daddies. As we laid down to sleep, we were surrounded by fortunes: love, family, and togetherness. We slept great.

## Monday, February 21, 2011

Since returning to our bed, Kel was getting much better sleep. At home, his appetite had dramatically increased. Sadly, neither the bed nor our home could ease his pain. Kel's mood fluctuated with his pain level, and the meds weren't effective unless he took more than suggested. He had four pills to maintain a tolerable level of pain, but he had another night and several hours of travel before he could get the necessary handwritten prescription from the Mayo Clinic. Kel was forced to tighten up on his meds. Patience was a virtue, but my patient was in pain and my inability to help him was driving me crazy. We found no other choice but to adapt and move forth.

I recalled a radio commercial I had heard years earlier: car care versus health care. The point of the commercial was that we tend to do whatever we need to keep our cars running, but we fill our bodies with garbage and run them down. Kelly and I were going to do everything to keep his body running smoothly, but we had to get past the bumps in the road.

## Tuesday, February 22, 2011

Sleepy-eyed, we arrived at the Mayo Clinic. The melanoma specialist awoke our tear ducts as we faced our reality. Up-front and honest, the doctor gave us specifics and facts regarding melanoma and Kelly's future. Melanoma is the rarest type of skin cancer but it causes the most deaths. Kel's case, like almost all others, was caused by ultra violet injury. His type of melanoma was so aggressive that if we had waited another three months, his outcome would have been dire. He would require frequent dermatology exams each year, for life. Radiation and other treatments were needed to assure all of the cancer was removed. Kel was advised to use sunscreen, stop using tanning beds, and avoid prolonged sun sessions. The doctor encouraged traveling to warm sunny locations but said to stay in the shade. It was a new lifestyle, which happened to be a healthier one. Back in our hotel room, we talked, cried, and crashed.

Upon waking, we went about life exactly the way we would on any other out-of-town day. We got washed up and went shopping. You can't keep a gay man down and out of a store for long. During our first stop, Kel's face was uncovered, and he exhibited confidence. I caught a woman staring, and I looked at Kel to see if he was aware of her; he was. He actually laughed at my physical reaction to her rudeness. Whenever Kel and I entered a room, I analyzed the setting because I wanted to feel safe and keep him safe. I was aware if others were talking about us, and Kelly used to be happily oblivious. I wanted him to remain unaffected by what others were saying, thinking, or looking at. As he shopped, face exposed, I told him I was proud. He laughed it off and said, "We're in Rochester. No one is going to see me here. Besides, they are used to seeing things like this." I agreed to disagree. Kel was right; we didn't see anyone we knew. But I believed Rochester wasn't used to seeing the happiness and internal light that Kelly possessed.

We got back in the car, and Kel said, "Today feels very normal." After hearing so much dark reality, his comment was music to my ears. We grabbed a bite to eat, and I asked how he felt about everything. He laughed and replied, "Next they'll tell me they need to remove a rib, and I'll say, 'Good, I always wanted to be smaller around my ribcage.' My T-shirts always show them." His response not only made me laugh, it made me think of every gay guy who wears overly tight tees ... including me. Our conversations remained light and lively as we talked about good times and planned future ones.

## Wednesday, February 23, 2011

We were leaving the Mayo Clinic with positivity and a lot of information. Kelly's melanoma type was aggressive (on the extreme side) and had invaded his skeletal muscle. Doctors didn't feel confident with just the removal. Therefore, once Kel's flap was secure, radiation would begin. We learned some facial nerves had to be removed during surgery, which explained the numbness Kel was experiencing throughout the right side of his face. Though areas were numb, movement and pressure on some of these locations caused excruciating pain, thus making it impossible for us to hug the way we were accustomed to. Kelly could finally remove the leg bandage and allow air time to dry up the wounds. There was some concern about the grayish areas on the arm graft, but Kelly was told to keep an eye on them, begin exercising his wrist, and report any problems. The doctor snipped many stitches around the flap and told us to keep swabbing the areas until the remaining stitches disappeared. Finally, Kel was given the okay to start brushing his teeth.

Back at home, I unpacked while Kel made his first shaving attempt since surgery. Because swelling had gone down, stitches within the facial hair areas were loose and protruding. I caught Kelly pulling, with tweezers, on a stitched knot, ready to snip it with scissors. I yelled, and he coaxed me into assisting him. My stomach churned with every tug and snip. Each fragment was pulled with ease, and surrounding skin had little or no attachment to them. After his shave, Kel really noticed the drastic changes that had taken place—happy, drastic healing changes. I was used to Kelly having facial hair, but his freshly shaven baby face allowed an amazing visual of how much the flap had taken on color and nestled with the adjoining skin.

Exhausted from the day, we found solace within the comforts of our bed. Kelly slept while I listened to him snore and talk in his sleep. This was the first time since surgery Kel was able to sleep lying flat and on his back, hence the snoring. I was happily listening because it meant pain was under control. Upon waking and feeling good, we took the bandage off his leg so it could air dry. Kel thought the whole thing stunk, literally. Nothing about these circumstances had smelled pleasant, and where smell lacked, the sight filled the void. It was the smell of healing, and we were visually witnessing the changes. We embraced it, were amazed by it, and tried to appreciate every minute of it.

It had been almost two weeks, and his teeth were still miraculously white. Kelly was reunited with his toothbrush. With a mouth full of foamy paste, he gushed, "Ohhhhh, this feels amazing! Just like when I first showered—wonderful." His word choices weren't typically part of his vocabulary. Kel was embracing and feeling every moment as if he were living them, like an Herbal Essences shampoo commercial. Kelly was alive, the most important fact.

**Kelly sent this e-mail on the twenty-third; his words depict humor and spirit.**

*Things are going as well as can be expected, and surprisingly, the days are flying by. Today was quite a lazy day, which included probably the most sleep yet. We did, however, get a chance to take Chaos for a walk, and afterward pick up some yummy junk food from Culver's for me. Joe took a little convincing to take me there as he is still attempting to get me on a health kick. Luckily, my pouting still works ha! Ha! Thanks for all your positive thoughts and prayers.*

*P.S. Thankfully we haven't gotten all the snow you guys got hit with, because I'm sure it would have put Joe over the edge.*

# Thursday, February 24, 2011

Kel's snoring was so loud, and he was mumbling things I couldn't understand. He used to stop my snoring by pushing me or scaring me awake, so I tried a gentle, engaging approach when I woke him. I touched his shoulder, and in his ear I asked, "What were you dreaming?"

He responded groggily, "Umm, I am dreaming a lot. I'm singing in my dreams." Kel's singing was a hair better than his snoring. He rolled onto his side, and I was spared his snoring, but I hoped the singing continued in his dreams.

Time flew whether we were having fun or not. The days were meshing into one, and our daily dealings, much like naps, were at our leisure. Kel was growing more tired and nauseous from the healing smells that surrounded him. His leg had become more painful since the bandage was removed, and rubbing healing ointment on it added to the discomfort. He was proactive with his finger and wrist motor skills, but he was unable to make a fist. When he tried to move his hand backward, he said it felt like the tendons were going to pop out of his wrist. The right side of his head was very sore, the result of the intense way doctors pushed on his face during his appointment. Each day, Kelly was independently accomplishing more: unscrewing a bottle of water, grinding pepper, locking our front door, changing his clothes. These were simple tasks for most, but he was unable to do them after his surgery. I had previously worked eight years with special education students, and where sympathy lacked, my support overflowed. This was the same way I tried to encourage Kelly. I also continued to nit-pick over little things, and Kel still pushed my buttons like no other. Each bickerfest was just as important as the happy, comforting ones and always ended with laughter. Not only did we challenge each other, we learned, grew, and loved more deeply.

After we returned home from our family walk, Chaos snuggled tightly between us while we watched a movie. The last three weeks had strengthened all of our relationships, and each bonding moment felt like a gigantic hug. Our heads were cocked toward one another, our feet touched as they rested on the coffee table, and we held hands while Chaos slept between us. From an aerial view we formed a heart. It may sound sappy, but my love for them heightened my awareness and I was diggin' it.

## Friday, February 25, 2011

It was a rather peaceful night for me, but Kel slept sporadically. Once I got out of bed, he sprawled out, taking full advantage of the space, and crashed for a few hours. Upon waking, he moved to the living room couch, and while I washed dishes and clothes, he napped with Chaos.

To my surprise, Kelly was feeling good, and pain was under control. He wanted to venture out of the house in search of an electric shaver, which was recommended by his doctor. He also needed a stool softener because the pain meds had a major binding effect. At one point in our shopping adventure, Kel walked toward me and I found myself staring and analyzing. The flap had really changed hues and now matched the tones of his face. After I shared my analysis, he found a mirror and acknowledged his reflection. "It doesn't look too bad." Kelly was getting his face out there, and I thought, *He is a tough MF!* I was proud of him. We were aware when a perplexed young girl gazed at his face. With confidence, he walked by her. As we shopped the aisles, Kelly requested we take our time because it felt really good to be out. At our final destination, Kel bought a tie for work. He had a goal and a purpose: get healthy and go back to work.

It was easy for me to look at every picture taken during this cancer journey and see Kel. What I saw when I looked at him transcended physical appearance. When we were in public, Kel attracted looks from outsiders who were curious by nature. Strangers observing the surface were missing Kel's inner beauty. Bystanders wondering about his scars were oblivious to the incredible strength it took to bear them. Onlookers who saw the flap were blind to his arm graft and leg wound. My personal challenge was to acknowledge and believe every stare or look was of compassion and concern. Every day was a continuum of understanding, smiles, and optimism.

**Kelly sent this e-mail to a friend on the twenty-fifth of February:**

*Words can't even begin to express my gratitude toward the love I have felt through this whole nightmare! Many of my emotions when first coming home after surgery were caused from relying on Joe to do everything! I always considered myself to be very independent, and when I couldn't even put on socks, it really got to me. As they say, time is a healer, and day by day, I'm once again becoming more independent, which is making me more positive.*

## Saturday, February 26, 2011

Happy Hour: 9:30 a.m. through 11:00 p.m. We visited, socialized, and damn, we were tired. Throughout the day, Kel made plenty of humorous remarks regarding his appearance.

I was concerned he might start believing what he was saying, so we frequently had conversations to ease my mind, which may have also reassured his. The outside resources of love, wishes, and prayers showcased the relations Kel had built and nurtured. This support system was a powerful source of strength and energy overflowing us with emotional wealth. Kelly and I were blessed and surrounded by an invisible barrier that we could feel. One benefit from the previous weeks of hell was our heightened awareness: we were good together and for one another, and love encompassed us.

## Monday, February 28, 2011

While I was in one of my accounts, a coworker approached and said, "I see it in your eyes ... some sadness." Her comment was filled with so much compassion and love, my eyes welled up. We were supported by so many individuals who wanted us to shine bright. They became a force helping us forge through. Going back to work permitted me to wrap my head around a few things, but time away from Kelly was time I constantly thought about him. I was protective and fully aware that being overly protective could become counterproductive. I also knew others words, actions, etc. could impact a person's thoughts, because they had affected mine in previous years. Many would have gone home, grabbed a computer, and looked up melanoma right after being diagnosed, but Kelly did not. The internet could have been a great resource, but I was proud that Kel realized some journeys needed to be taken alone for the very simple fact that each of us differs in exceptional ways. The way he coped, healed, and lived was his to experience in his own unique way. Reading others' scenarios on the internet could have tainted the situation rather than allow his thoughts, feelings, and awareness to blossom. I wanted Kelly to discover and advance with confidence and assurance, without worry or words of caution. I appreciated brutal honesty and facts as long as the intent was to positively expand the state of mind or encourage the belief in possibility. I wasn't in denial. There were miracles happening every day, and meeting Kelly was one of mine. No matter what the odds, which are solely based on an average, we are all special and here to write our own story, not live someone else's.

**On February twenty-eighth, Kelly posted a supplemental paragraph under Basic Info on his Facebook page:**

*I really have grown to love life! It has dealt me a fair hand, and I don't take things for granted. I always stand by the phrase, "You get what you give."*

*As many of you are aware, the previous paragraph was written when I first signed up with FB. Now, after recently being diagnosed with melanoma cancer, my thoughts are, WHAT THE F#$% was I thinking! Although I will grow through this and someday learn to love life again, I wouldn't wish this upon anyone! Also, I have learned from this that pretty cars, beautiful homes, and money mean very little. Please take the extra time to cherish your family and friends, because in the end, they mean so much more than anything! One more thing, the word love is very easy to say, so make sure those special people in your life know exactly how you feel! Enough mush for now.*

# Tuesday, March 1, 2011

It was late evening and I was jealous of those who were already in bed. I felt challenged as I stepped back into work mode, and though I was going through the motions, my head was spinning. Kel's schedule was completely out of whack (eating salmon patties at five in the morning), and it was affecting any regularity I had. While I was at work, he was sleeping most of the time, and that gave me some peace of mind but also added to our irregularities.

In his honor, Kel's coworkers decided they wanted and needed to have a benefit. Several other friends attended the first meeting, and I observed individuals from different aspects of our lives band together for the guy I loved. My happy-go-lucky face was a front because inside I was welled up with gratitude and appreciation. Weeks before this meeting, Kel and I discussed whether we should do an event like this. At the time, we felt a benefit would make us feel awkward, but we also believed his cancer concerns were almost over. We were both stubborn and didn't like to ask for help; pride sometimes interfered with our needs. We were grateful our loved ones took it upon themselves and began to put an event together.

Kel's journey began with "You have melanoma," and the road continued to be challenging during the healing process. Throughout the sadness and gloom, there were so many awakenings and revelations that accelerated personal growth; it was amazing. Our friends were having a benefit for Kel, and neither of us had experienced people rallying for us and lifting our spirits with laughter and helping hands. Was it always this way? Were we finally awake? I was aware that nothing was the same and it never would be, but I didn't want to go back. Kel and I had grown and we were better than ever.

> "It's going to take more than cancer to keep
> this queen from being fabulous!"
> - Kelly Boedigheimer

## Wednesday, March 2, 2011

Kel showered, changed his dressings, swabbed his stitches, cleaned the house, and made the bed. I could have cried like an overbearing mother, because he was beginning to need me less. His successes were awesome, and I was proud that he was taking control. I knew he still needed me, and I needed him.

While I worked, Kel went to his car appointment; no drugs were taken before he sat behind the wheel. His vehicle, like Chaos, was his baby and it needed some TLC. Kelly was well-known by the serviceman, who took one look and said, "Geez, Kelly, I can only imagine what the other guy looks like." Kelly shared his story, and the guy probably felt like an ass. But where would we be if people didn't open up and say what they felt or shared what they saw? This guy gave Kelly an opportunity to share his story, and I believed that guy went home and shared it with others. Communication—what better way to unite, teach, and learn?

In January, Kel cried out, "Why my face? Why?" Yet in March, he walked tall and proud, ready to share his story. Kel was on one hell of a journey, and I wasn't sure if he realized how much he had grown. He was still vain, and he panned numerous post-surgery photos before approving two to be placed on Caring Bridge.

As we settled in for the evening, Kelly gave me details regarding his arm mishaps. Per doctors' instructions Kel was told to let water run over the graft and lightly pat it dry. Two days prior, as the water washed over it, Kel rubbed part of the graft and apparently the skin rolled along with it. As he spoke, my stomach churned, and then I yelled, reciting what the doctors said. Kel was mad for a moment, but he knew I was right. He said when he removed the dressing this morning, quite a bit of skin had stuck to it and smelled like a rotting corpse. I was just about to lecture when he assured me there was new pink-colored flesh under the skin that came off. All I could say was, "Oh God, I hope so." Healing was crucial for his arm mobility, and being told that skin rolled and pulled off didn't make me feel warm and fuzzy inside. Kel was feeling good and showed no visual concerns over what he experienced, and I could only follow his lead.

## Thursday, March 3, 2011

While I was working, a dude full of pep and positive energy was bouncing around the aisles. My first thought was, *What is he on?* He began to talk and mentioned what a beautiful day it was and how he was happy to be alive. I, of course, pointed out that it was freakin' cold and not exactly beautiful. He said, "It's awesome out there. We are one day closer to spring, and that feels great." Normally I would have thought he was a whack job, but as he walked away, I appreciated the imprint he left. Our brief encounter had purpose, and this dude helped me gain some perspective about the previous night.

The previous night before bed, Kel told me that everything was happening during the perfect time of year. He disliked winter and usually kept himself inside until the weather was warmer.

The moment he shared his feelings about winter, he was hit with the reality of an altered spring and summer. He grieved, "I won't be able to do any of my favorite things. No lying in the sun, no tanning bed, no vacation for who knows how long. I won't want to go out on the weekends because I won't feel good about myself." I wanted Kel to figure out why these statements manifested, but I wasn't sure if I should let him continue or intercede. At times, Kel's mind would write the story before he actually lived it. His spring and summer woes were perfect examples. Kel wanted to roll with the punches, and most of the time he did, but sometimes he forgot to punch back. His life was already different, but different was only a negative when he forgot to be positive.

That dude helped me realize I had the choice to be happy or go about my day as if he never emotionally reached me. Observing him made it clear I wanted to find happiness within every moment. Though our internal bodies functioned without mental or physical control, our attitude toward life was completely under our authority. I felt alive inside and out as I grasped the riches of life. I was excited to go home and share this occurrence with Kelly because it was about living now.

Lying in bed, we shared details about our day and had heart-to-heart conversations. All the while we were conversing, Kel's toes were squeezing my toes. In sync with his final toe squeeze, he said, "I'm making love to you." We busted up laughing ... it was so random and right in the middle of a serious talk. Joy was always within reach, and Kel understood that more than me.

# Chapter Three

## Radiation

### Friday, March 4, 2011

The beginning of our three-and-a-half-hour road trip to the Rochester Mayo Clinic in Minnesota felt very typical. Kel was ragging on my driving, and in return I threatened to throw him on the hood of the car for the remainder of the ride. Arriving safe and sound, we met with the radiologist and were told Kel's type of melanoma was very strange in behavior. They called it an intransient metastasis and believed it started on his face, with intentions of going elsewhere. She suggested a radiation treatment that was fairly new, aggressive, and had positive results to date. Because facial radiation requires precautions and safety, Kelly was encouraged to have the five treatments at the Mayo Clinic. After discussing the many possible side effects, permanent hair loss became the hardest one for me to accept. I began to question how much more Kel would have to endure. No one truly knew what was going to go on within Kel's body, so I began to envision every positive source teaming with the energy put from our loved ones clobbering the bad guys.

The previous weeks had passed swiftly, and actions put forth had been quick. Every doctor seemed to have connections, and they used them to get us what they felt we needed. Before proceeding with radiation, Kel was required to have a mask made (which was used to place him in the proper position for every treatment), have a dental exam, meet a dietician, and speak with a social worker. We moved along nicely from appointment to appointment, gathering more knowledge and information.

Leaving the Mayo Clinic wasn't great, but it supplied us with food for thought. All I ever had to go on was what I saw and heard or what Kel shared with me. I wanted to cheer him on and support him, which could have gone wrong at any moment, and basically it did. Kelly yelled, "Just shut up for the rest of the trip until we get to your parents' house! I am tired of talking about me, me, me. I don't want to talk about me anymore. I want to talk about anything else." Kel decided when he wanted to talk and to whom he wanted to talk and how long he wanted to talk. I was trying to keep up with e-mails, texts, phone calls, and questions from every direction, and they were all about him. I understood where he was coming from because I too had been living and breathing a life that revolved around him. Our silence was a result of numerous discussions involving Kel's prognosis, but the final straw was a conversation on hair loss due to radiation. I took the "let's be optimistic" approach while Kel accepted the "what would most likely happen" statistic. We were told some patients never lose their hair, and I wanted to believe that Kel would be one of them. There was a minute chance of facial hair regrowth after radiation, and that was all I needed to hear to proceed with optimism. As I spoke about the hair growth potential, Kel accused me of caring about the way he looked rather than the fact he was alive. He said I was stressing him out and being negative by thinking he could regrow hair. Once upon a time, Kel told me if anything tragic had happened to him or his face that he would rather be dead, and those comments directly impacted the positivity I was trying to instill in him on this drive. My intentions were good, but he obviously didn't view them the way they were meant. He didn't seem open, and I felt he denied every good wish, thought, or prayer I was putting forth. Could he receive? He appeared to be closed off and guarded, yet acted as if he had positive knowledge.

Kel was a supporter of everyone, and yet when it came to himself, he could fall short. He said I was putting pressure on him regarding his recovery, but he had done better than all of the medical expectations thus far. I finally drove in silence and realized my main and only focus had been him. I wasn't really sure what my focus was four weeks prior. We arrived at my folks' place, and he said, "Now wasn't that nice?" If anyone thought Kel and I a picture-perfect couple, getting along every waking moment, he needed his head examined. We were like everyone else, and every day had a learning curve.

Soon we were back on the road and headed for our next stop, Kel's folks. All was good before entering his parents' home because we cleared the air by quickly explaining our points of view. This visit went well, but as we were getting ready to leave, Kel shared my hair growth optimism, and I felt mocked as he and his family laughed. We got back in the car, and I told him I wanted complete silence until we got home. This time was spent processing and collecting my thoughts.

It's undeniable cancer affects every aspect of a relationship. I really bugged the shit out of Kelly, and he bugged the shit out of me. There were some days I just wasn't going to like him, and there were days he was going to hate my guts! We both forgot we were a team fighting for the exact same thing, and some days we needed to fight together but in different cars.

## Saturday, March 5, 2011

Go figure: every dream I had involved Kel. I wasn't sure how long the dreams would continue, but they only made it more apparent there was no escape from this reality. I was fortunate to have people, including Kel, keeping me grounded, because they permanently halted a major breakdown. Though I felt rested and it was a new day, I had to mentally revisit the previous day because there were many positives despite our differences.

On Friday, while Kel had his mask made for radiation, I was outside in the waiting area, where a young guy from Missouri and his two companions sat. The guy was waiting to have his mask made, so we shared our cancer journeys. He was diagnosed with melanoma over one year prior. While he was getting a haircut, the stylist cut into an unknown mass on the back of his head. It bled profusely, and he was sent to the hospital for stitches and testing. Every lymph node removed tested positive, and he was classified as a Stage Four melanoma patient. This was his third melanoma bout, and he explained, "The human head has many vessels where cancer can hide and go undetected by an MRI or CAT scan." Doctors did their best to remove every known cancerous area, but they were watching him closely. This guy was also giving himself chemo shots, which would boost healthy cells and prevent melanoma from spreading to other areas throughout his body. He had researched other hospitals throughout the States, and the Mayo Clinic was the only facility offering this form of chemo, which was more advanced and efficient, and less invasive. The shots were doing exactly what doctors had wanted, and the cancer had been contained within his head. Kelly's doctors had planned on starting him on these shots as soon as his radiation was completed. There sat this guy, a positive source of information, and I felt Kel was right where he needed to be.

Kelly shared his experience of the mask-making, which is called the simulation process. They laid him on an uneven bed, and he held that position for fifteen minutes, which became painful. A very wet, warm, tight mesh was placed over his head and shoulders as several hands pushed and contoured the mesh to his face. It dried so quickly that they had to do it more than once in order to get it perfect. After it dried, the mask was used to lock him in place on the bed, and it pulled his head back so tight that it almost hurt. He tried to open his eyes and was partially successful, squinting with one. To me, this sounded like a true test of trust and overcoming claustrophobia. He would have a blocker on his tongue to avoid radiating it. Just like during a dentist visit, saliva pools in the back of the throat and triggers the gag reflex. During the fifteen minutes of radiation, he would have to discover ways to cope with this awkwardness. On the flip side, we had learned one saliva gland was removed during his surgery, which meant he would be dealing with 50 percent less spit. Kelly also got a tattoo, the most expensive one he'd ever receive. The center of his chest was shaved and ink was dropped where hair once was. With a needle in her hand, the medical specialist pierced Kelly's skin, making tiny circles so the ink could enter. This tattoo would be used as a marker in order to place Kel in the same position for radiation each time.

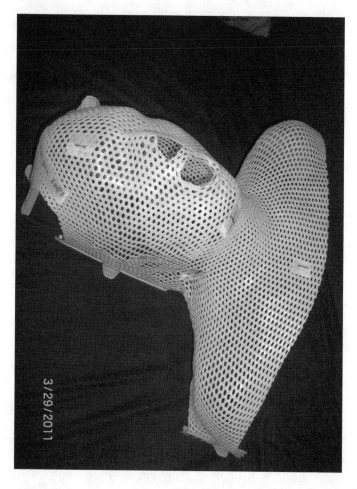

3/29/2011

Throughout the hustle and bustle, we shared sarcastic banter. While walking into the Mayo Clinic, Kel had a great idea. "How would I look if I let my hair grow down around my chin on both sides?" He positioned his hands the way the hair would flow. We laughed, and I asked him if he really wanted to know what he would look like.

Of course he did, to which I said, *"Alone!"* Damn, did he laugh, and that made me laugh.

Later the same day, we were in the radiology department. Checked in and seated in the waiting area, Kel said, "I was apprehensive about coming here because I wasn't sure what kind of things we would see."

Everyone there happened to be average, young and old, and I looked at Kel and said, *"Surprise,* you're the scariest one in here." We laughed so hard that tears streamed down our cheeks.

**Kelly sent this e-mail on March seventh, and I found it to be a humorous addition.**

*Did Joe ever tell you about the mask fitting? Crazy, crazy, crazy! It took them three tries to get mine perfectly snug, and I now know exactly how a frozen turkey feels in its mesh casing. Well just after the fitting, I returned to the waiting area, where Joe and a few others were waiting. Needless to say Joe had some chuckles over what had happened to my hair during the fitting process. Let's just say it was the worst bed head in the back while the front was sticking straight up. I definitely learned I will not be putting any product in my hair prior to any future treatments.*

## Sunday, March 6, 2011

I questioned if this awful game came with a manual. The rules seemed to change day by day, and even if we didn't want to play, we had to. It was like picking an emotion out of a hat—random and unpredictable. This was a day of contemplation and distance, and we both needed time to process on our own. But at night, we played by our rules.

Kel was sporadic with thoughts, words, and decisions, and he felt the drugs affected the way he focused. I could tell the anti-depressants altered his natural coping strategies, but my observations were unimportant compared to Kel's need for them. We had a serious conversation, and he confessed his pain never completely went away. He couldn't imagine living life with pain that never ceased, and he admitted, with a sigh of relief, that the pain was much better. I could see that he was taking fewer pills, but I had no idea what pains he was living with or had lived through. I wondered if he was harboring troubling feelings or thoughts, and I wanted him to share so I could offer comfort. I couldn't take it away and I couldn't feel it for him; I didn't see what he saw when he looked at himself, and I couldn't force him to hear me when I tried to comfort him. How could there be a manual? I could write *How To Be a Gay*, and try to explain every detail, but until you live it, words could never define it.

Company arrived at 7:00 p.m., and after they left, Kel said, "This was the first real normal evening we have had." We had a couple of drinks, conversations rolled, and future plans were discussed. Living in the now required us to look at future events in order to pull us through tough spells. Having house guests gave us opportunities to converse about topics other than cancer and melanoma. Kel confessed he was drawn to his friends and family and wanted to be around them because they weren't pushing him like I was. My initial thought was, *Amen and thank you*, because as his partner, I felt I needed to encourage and push. I knew he resented me at times, but his best interest was all I ever had in mind, even if he didn't see it that way. He may have mocked me for thinking he was a special patient or for saying anything was possible (even when others were saying it was impossible), but if there wasn't a thing called a miracle, the word would have never been created. I fell in love with someone from Cloquet, Minnesota, moved away from my incredible family and friends, and lived happily for thirteen years. That was a miracle.

## Monday, March 7, 2011

It was our thirteenth anniversary, and we spent the day doing things that made us feel and look better, and then we lounged together. After getting a haircut, Kel looked in a mirror and said, "Oh, this feels so good. When I look in the mirror, I see myself again." He looked great, but more important, he looked like he felt great. There was hardly a moment when cancer wasn't part of our daily life, and witnessing a boost in Kel's self-esteem was extremely gratifying.

Kelly divulged that he feared the tumor would grow back, and I had the same fear. Previous attempts to remove it had failed, and we had become jaded by those misfortunes. It was comparable to a car accident: the crash remains in the mind, and paranoia strikes when you're behind the wheel. Every day brought a greater sense of trust and contentment. I didn't want to wish our time away, but I was anxious to get past the physical and mental trials and tribulations. It was up to us to avoid being ruled by what-ifs and find our way back to our comfortable lives.

# Tuesday, March 8, 2011

Kelly's internal pain was greatly reduced, but his mouth soreness remained. I could see the swelling had gone down in his right cheek-bone region, but his jaw was stiff and his speech was tight-lipped. He mumbled as he approached me with the digital camera, telling me I could add one leg and one arm picture to the Caring Bridge site. I was impressed by this personal growth and willingness, and I believed sharing the process entirely and whole-heartedly was beneficial for others. Family and friends would now have more visuals to help them grasp our truth.

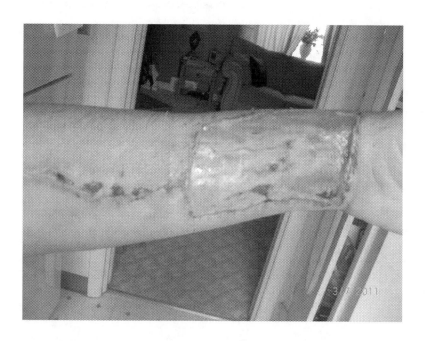

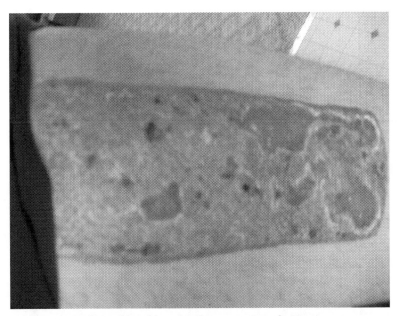

**Kelly referred to his leg as a Steak-Umm.**

Every day, Kel was picking up around the house, fixing the bed, taking care of his own wraps and bandages, and staying current with messaging. His limitations were never my focus because I was only concerned with helping him build upon his abilities. Kelly was doing exercises to gain strength in his hand and regain flexibility in his wrist. He would stand in front of a mirror, using his right hand to gently push his left hand back as far as he could. Though he could curl all of his fingers and was almost able to form a fist, he voiced concerns over his inability to bend his thumb. While he was working on his hand movement, he was able to bend his thumb ever so slightly. I could see excitement in his eyes, and it was a moment to be excited about. I wanted him to pat himself on the back, but instead his mind traveled back one month, when bending his thumb wasn't a concern or an issue, and he downplayed his achievement. I watched Kel's face go from extreme happiness to sadness, and I felt my heart wrench for him. His thumb moved for the first time because he made it move; that was huge no matter how small he thought it was. I began to realize how much I took for granted, and it became important for both of us to find a new appreciation for everything. These challenges brought more awareness, and this was our new reality.

## Wednesday, March 9, 2011

As healing continued, stitches were being pushed from Kel's face, and he escorted some of them out with tweezers. I did a light tapping test on the lower half of his face and asked him to tell me when he could feel it. He couldn't, but there were random moments when some feeling would creep back in. His leg had two small areas that were still very tender, which Chaos had jumped on a few times. It was a vicious cycle for Kelly, because he would yell at Chaos for causing him pain, and then he'd feel bad and try to comfort him. His arm was showing the quickest signs of recovery. Kelly told me that he didn't want to see a physical therapist and was hoping to regain arm, wrist, and hand mobility on his own. One day, Kel noticed an increase in overall flexibility and was finally appreciating the now rather than reflecting on the past.

## Thursday, March 10, 2011

Getting back to work and finding my competitive edge felt good. This was my longest work day since I had returned, and I chatted with Kel a few times. Every time I called, he was a busy bee. During one conversation, he confessed he had made my favorite Kelly meal: lasagna. He cooked! He washed the dishes, and when I walked through the front door, he was organizing one of his junk drawers. If I had grabbed a Magic 8 Ball and asked, "Is Kelly proud of himself and his accomplishments?" the response would have been, "All signs point to *yes*." Loving life was the usual aura Kelly emitted, and it was apparent this day. I wasn't sure what feelings and emotions I was experiencing: pride, joy, happiness, relief, hope, love. I had never been more aware that Kel's state of mind directly affected mine. We rolled through the worst together, we wanted the best for each other, and we continued growing and learning about one another.

## Friday, March 11, 2011

Two Mayo Clinic visits ago, I watched a doctor tug on some of Kelly's stitches and cut off the excess. Some people can leave a zit alone and others need to pick it. I admit I'm a picker, but Kelly was worse. Kel had previously talked me into assisting him with protruding stitches, but he also went at it alone. He was cleaning his facial wounds, and I noticed blood on his shirt and in the sink, so I questioned what had happened. He assured me there was nothing to be concerned about but later confessed he had pulled out a stitch and a flow of blood followed. I also noticed his leg was bleeding, and he said, "Sometimes when I sit, the skin stretches and cracks, and that is probably what happened." After he chuckled, he fessed up: it itched, and he scratched. One hand or two, it didn't matter, because he would find a way to itch or pick.

Kel knew I was going to nag, and I knew he would eventually admit the truths. Humor laced our predictable behavior and brought us laughter. We witnessed a spectrum of emotional and physical healing. Love and support surrounded us every step of the way.

## Saturday, March 12, 2011

Our mailbox was flooded with Mayo bills, future appointment instructions, and an envelope containing Kel's surgical info with the findings to date. Reading detailed information created an awakening different from what we had already lived through. For example: Kelly's first mass removal regrew to the same size within two and a half weeks. These written words scared the shit out of me, and I became aware of why the doctors had the sense of urgency and fear. However, reading the leg graft stats made the sight more amazing. Kel's leg was healing, and flesh tones were now dominant. It was exciting. His wound would soon be a memory. Kelly's only complaint was that it itched like heck. Sometimes ignorance is bliss; therefore, I questioned whether I should continue reading ... I did. *A tiny nodular opacity projected over the base of Kel's heart* was documented, and my mind flooded with questions and concerns. Though it was never previously mentioned, I wondered if it could be melanoma.

I looked over at Kel and told him how good he looked. I wasn't by his side to bullshit or pacify him; I was there to support him the way a life partner could. I hoped Kel heard my sincerity, but instead he took my words and made fun of them. He said, "Post-surgery I look good, but pre-surgery I don't." His comment broke my heart, and I explained the meaning of my words. I saw him every day and I didn't have any illusions as to what he looked like, nor did I speak with rose-colored glasses on. I spoke what I felt and saw. Kel wasn't ready to believe what I said, but I continued to show my love for him was unaffected.

## Monday, March 14, 2011

It was a sunny, dry drive as we headed to the Mayo Clinic for the first radiation treatment. Kel was anxious for numerous reasons but mostly because he didn't know what to expect. He checked in at 11:45 a.m., and by 12:15 p.m., radiation was finished. I was sitting in the waiting room when Kel walked over to me and said, "How do you like the dots on my forehead?" The mask used to strap him down left tiny circles all over his face and exhibited the amount of pressure Kel endured as he was locked into place. He also said, "That was a piece of cake—super simple." I was so happy things went well and he only had four treatments left.

One hour after radiation, Kel experienced some discomfort, and the pain was continually increasing. He told me his face felt like taffy—tight, but as if his facial muscles were being pulled out. Two hours after radiation, he was miserable and we both were feeling helpless. Talking was painful and his overall pain level was higher than his surgical hospital stay. As the pain increased, he said, "It feels like someone is continuously beating my face with a bat." Nothing had prepared us for the excruciating pain Kel was feeling, so I called the radiologist. After she apologized for not forewarning us about this side effect that 15 percent of patients experience, she explained Kel's salivary gland was swollen, irritated, and needed help (via lemon drops) to promote saliva. She guaranteed Kel would not experience this pain after his other treatments and he would feel better within twenty-four hours.

After buying some lemon drops, Kelly was desperately trying to find a comfortable, pain-free position as he squirmed in his seat. One and a half hours later, we finally arrived home. Before getting into bed, he said, "If I have this kind of pain, I won't be able to finish this! I'm going to sleep for a little bit in hopes I wake up hungry." I needed him to stick with it and get healthy, but I didn't know how to silence his pain. After he woke, Kel was feeling better and had an appetite. There was still pain, but he had some control over it; numbness replaced areas where feeling was beginning to reemerge, and facial swelling had increased. These side effects crept in quicker than either of us had expected, and as much as we wanted to put on a brave front, it scared us.

It had been a long time since I had experienced a gnawing feeling in my gut that I couldn't wait to expel. This reality was heartbreaking at times, but I continued to believe the pains were part of the full recovery. I was anxious for the radiation chapter to be complete because it felt like we would have closure on this cancer. After a physical and emotional day, I felt confident I would hear Kel snore; nothing would have made me happier.

## Tuesday, March 15, 2011

Just like the swelling, spirits were back up. Kel's pain was completely under control, and snoring throughout the night confirmed he slept. Even though I had to work, I constantly bugged Kel with texts and calls just to make sure everything was going right. He ignored a couple of my calls, which, oddly enough, was a good sign. Like a post-surgery flashback, swelling from radiation made chewing and talking difficult. Though his appearance was similar to weeks earlier, Kel was able to eat and swallow with little difficulty. His next treatment was his major worry. He was very swollen, and he feared the potential pain and pressure that he may experience from the radiation mask. I did my best to promote rest, relaxation, and absorption of positive energy.

## Wednesday, March 16, 2011

When Kel ate mac and cheese at 5:00 a.m., I realized any regularity we had was gone. Our meals together were random, our schedules were in sync as much as they could be, and our security with one another was as tight as ever. I loved the fact I could pick on Kel and he would pick right back: bicker, nag, etc. We needled each other just like kids at play.

This morning, Kel took his finger and shoved it in my face. We weren't sure if radiation singed the stitches that remained inside his mouth, but a loose portion of them was escorted out by his tongue and sat on the tip of this finger that was inches from my eyes. Then he showed me his arm, which looked damn good. It was apparent he found comfort in the healing progress but feared the return of any discomfort. Moments of being pain-free were tainted by lurking potential pain.

Many loved ones were beginning to express concerns regarding my health, but by Kel's side was where I felt in control, secure, and safe. For me, the unhealthy thing would have been trying to attempt anything other than what felt natural. The reality following the first treatment was hell because I had to witness Kel in pain, but there were never any questions, wonders, or hesitations about being beside him. As emotionally unpredictable as the circumstances were, our love for one another gave us the courage and strength to move forward. Just like walking, we did it because we had someplace we wanted to go. We didn't pick this detour in our life, but for some reason we were there. There was only one way to go, and we moved with confidence, hope, love, and pride. The only way to follow our path was to take the lead.

## Thursday, March 17, 2011

Picture it: you're lying on a hard bed, tranquil scenes are floating above, music plays softly to relax and soothe your body, mind, and soul. The mask that covers your head and shoulders is clamped down so tight you are afraid to open your eyes out of fear you may not be able to close them again. You can't resist trying to take a peek at what is going on. One eye opens partially as your eyelashes act like bangs. How is the view? Your other eye is open, but the holey mask distorts your vision and you struggle to view the tranquil scene. At least you still have the soothing music. *Beeeeeep... radiation starts.* It is so loud. Finally in a zone, unfortunately the spit starts pooling in the back of your throat. With the tongue guard contraption in your mouth, you panic and question if you'll be able to swallow. You can. Then you relax.

After radiation, Kelly walked into the waiting room, and the right side of his face and forehead looked like a golf ball but with embossed dimples. Humor dripped from his words as he shared this experience, and then he said, "It was a piece of cake." I felt panic-stricken from the horrific details, and I thought, *It sounded like hell and yet you act like it was better than getting your face washed with your mother's spit rag.* Kel still felt like he had been punched in the face and muscles were being pulled out, but round two was much better.

Before driving home, we had a surgical follow-up visit and an appointment with a dietician. Kel learned he no longer needed to wear his arm brace, and he was advised to indulge in comfort foods (fast food restaurants, shakes, chocolate) in order to maintain his weight. It was a cloudy day, but sunshine was all around.

## Friday, March 18, 2011

Treatment number two may have been better but Kel was experiencing new pain, sensations and familiar emotions. He said he felt like a fish being carried under the gill because of a constant pulling feeling. He had cold water and almost screamed as it flowed over his teeth. His face had so much pressure from swelling, it felt like a rock behind his skin. His bottom lip and inner cheek were numb, and he had to be cautious when he ate so he wouldn't chew on them. When he told me he felt like he could cry, I wanted him to let the tears flow. Tears are cleansing, and we both needed to cleanse.

Present circumstances could have caused us to feel defeated, but we weren't. Pain (emotional or physical) of any kind was just that: a pain. We were awake to the fact our experiences were part of the process, but it was still Kel's prerogative to kick and scream, sit and cry, sleep and dream, or eat and shit. Every single moment expanded who we were and the capabilities we had. I think Kel was feeling like he had been pushed to the brink, but I knew he had more within.

I believed one day we would reenter our comfy routine of life, and little accomplishments wouldn't feel like huge successes that needed to be shared. But during this time, all successes and setbacks were backed with love. "No one fights alone" was a slogan I discovered cancer survivors, fighters, and supporters used. I felt the truth behind the words.

## Saturday, March 19, 2011

Kel needed lots of rest because every activity quickly exhausted him. He had a healthy appetite, and per dietician's orders, Kel was eating high-calorie meals. It was difficult to support these eating habits, but I was happy his desire for food was thriving. For the first time, Kelly's sweet tooth had surpassed mine, and we purchased several junk food items to guarantee weight stability.

Kelly wore jeans for the first time, and all of his unused medical supplies were put away and out of view. It was one of our most normal, familiar-feeling days because Kel was in his everyday clothes and our home lacked any visual reminders of the reality we wanted to forget.

Yesterday taught us, and we utilized the knowledge today. Today was an opportunity to move forward. Tomorrow was unwritten but a guarantee it would be different from today.

## Sunday, March 20, 2011

Kel and I chatted about his pain, and he described it as agitating, annoying, painful, etc. Days earlier, I found myself imagining a pain-free future because I hated when he hurt. As Kel's healing continued, my own regimen was slowly returning. We had adapted and learned many things, but there was so much more to be taught. I witnessed Kelly's ownership of this life experience, and I believed he would use every opportunity to rise up, grow, and surpass expectations. If he thought or felt moving forward was too scary or difficult, acknowledgement of his surrounding support rekindled his inner strength and became a driving force. Kelly's cancer was not a solo mission because the power of many were battling and conquering it together. Our future was going to consist of a new course, new experiences, and new challenges. Everything was new and an opportunity to start fresh.

## Monday, March 21, 2011

It was another day trip, for treatment number three at the Mayo Clinic, and Kel slept most of the way. Kelly had been experiencing upper back pain, and it was interfering with his sleep, so I was relieved he was getting some rest. We learned surgeons had to cut into Kel's neck muscle tissue in order to remove lymph nodes, and back pains were normal side effects. We had no idea Kel's neck and shoulder movements were at risk until we heard a story about a woman who, after a surgery like Kel's, didn't perform her daily exercises and could no longer turn her head. Therapy was no longer in question, so we made an appointment.

Radiation to Kel was like pot to a pothead; the munchies appeared to be a side effect. Kelly was weighed before every appointment, and he had actually gained a little weight. I was relieved his appetite remained intact and eating difficulties were nonexistent. Kel said this was his most comfortable treatment but he could tell the intensity had increased. He was warned about the side effects (mouth sores, swallowing issues, etc.), and pain control was pills away. Kelly seemed confident in the means to keep the pain at bay. He was as comfortable as one might expect and sleepier than ever before, showcasing Jekyll and Hyde moments, but every bit of his quirky, crazy self was shining through.

"The radiation has kicked my ass thus far, but the nice thing is that I will be done with it for two whole weeks before the benefit." - Kelly

## Tuesday, March 22, 2011

Kelly's appetite was intact but his energy lacked. His ambition lasted briefly and then he was down for the count: thirty minutes on and then three hours of recovery. When he felt energized, it seldom lasted long enough to complete what he began. His frustration was obvious, and despite needing breaks, he was adamant in finishing what he started.

The incision in front of Kel's right ear was covered in dried blood, and he noticed leakage from the incision under his chin. We assumed the swelling and pressure from radiation had caused old wounds to reopen. It was easy to identify the areas where radiation was targeted because they were hard to the touch. Even though there was major swelling from radiation, the flap had decreased and was now one with the surrounding areas. I wanted to keep touching his face and arm. The grafted skin on his arm had a shellacked appearance and was so soft, but it was highly sensitive. If I touched the base of the graft, Kel could feel the sensation throughout its entirety. I was careful as

I assisted him with wrist movements, and obviously he refused to play mercy or bloody knuckles.

I found myself nagging Kel more and more, but each nag was doused with assurance coming from a concerned, loving place. His ears had no choice but to hear my pleas, and his mouth unleashed what he really thought. We were a team.

## Wednesday, March 23, 2011

*Hey Everyone,*

*It's me ... Kelly. As you have all figured out, Joe is an excellent writer along with being a "tell all" kind of person. This, of course, doesn't leave much for me to say and most definitely has its pros and cons, just like everything.*

*Pros: He keeps everyone well-informed and occasionally humored!*

*Cons: He tells certain things I'd rather were kept within our home, and when I'm feeling better, he's gonna get it!*

*Anyway, I just wanted to reach out and thank all of you once again for the amount of support you have given us through this journey. You have all made me open my eyes, mind, and heart, and I know in the end that I will walk away a more sincere, caring, and overall better person.*

*I wish you all the VERY BEST!*

*Love,*
*Kelly*

# Thursday, March 24, 2011

We arrived for radiation twenty-five minutes early and everything was ready for Kelly. I appreciated the efficiency, but I sensed apprehension from Kel before this treatment. I tend to avoid things that cause me pain or discomfort (regardless if they are meant to help). Therefore, Kel's hesitancy came as no surprise. While he was in radiation, I experienced a teary moment. From within the waiting room, I heard the clanking of a large bell followed by cheers and applause. It was the bell ringer's last treatment and his first day of a new chapter. There was a tremendous amount of energy within that room, and I became aware of my desires and hopes. As my tears continued to flow, I acknowledged I still had a lot of emotional releasing to do.

Kel hit the sack the moment we were home and remained there for hours. I assumed he would rise when he was hungry, as his appetite was good. However, his throat was becoming tender and the swelling was no better. Thankfully, the painkillers were keeping him comfortable and relaxed. Before Kel woke, I did some soul-searching.

Caretaker: social welfare, see also carer a person who takes care of a vulnerable person, often a close relative. Definition number three taken from Dictionary.com.

I was referred to as Kelly's caretaker, and though I appreciated every positive comment, I despised the word. Kel was vulnerable, as was I, and we supported and assisted each other during this time. Referring to me as Kel's caretaker felt like it put him at a solo disadvantage, but we were a team. His strength and perseverance had guided me through this process as if he were *my* caretaker. It was a word that made me feel as if my relationship with Kel was changed even though I believed we were united equals. The word *caretaker* took the equal out of our equation, and that bothered me. I wanted to shout, "Kelly is strong, brave, stubborn, independent, and capable. I am fortunate to be his partner!"

***Kelly sent this e-mail on March twenty-fourth:***

*I really, really appreciate being able to hear about others and, for moments, forget about me (it's exhausting)! As you're aware, some individuals post often on Caring Bridge and have described some of the pain that others have endured during radiation. Now I'm not really a person who agrees with the saying "misery loves company." However, it is simply nice to be able to relate. I feel I may understand a bit better regarding what others went through with treatments. Anyway, thus far, the magic date for my return (for work) is set for May 9, but I'm crossing my fingers for a quicker recovery and a faster return. In closing, please know that I'm so appreciative of everyone for their help with everything, and I look forward to seeing many at the benefit.*

# Friday, March 25, 2011

We reached a point where I was able to talk about Kel's sleeping habits rather than his progress because he was asleep more than awake. Sitting quietly was once difficult for Kelly, but any amount of conversation seemed to take a toll on his energy level. I was waking him to give him his meds or to get him to eat. He was still enjoying high-calorie meals, and thankfully, any potential throat issues seemed unlikely. There was one positive: his old Hoover vacuum style of eating had become a normal chewing pace and we were finishing meals at the same time.

Sleep was definitely a healing force regarding his face, arm, and leg; they were looking great. Kel's focus was divided, and I hoped he was finding time to appreciate the results. I realized he was tired, and I could see the pain his arm exercises induced, but I wanted to scream at him until he successfully completed them. I wasn't sure if the high medication doses were lessening his arm mobility concerns, but I was extremely concerned. It was frustrating for both of us.

In order to defuse and refocus, I wrote, "Life always has something to look forward to, if you allow yourself to acknowledge it. I don't expect miracles but I do believe in them. Some good things may come to those who wait, but if you wait, some good things might pass you by. You have control over your life; it's just easier to act like you don't. If you want to succeed, then do the work and achieve. What have you done today to make you feel proud?"

## Saturday, March 26, 2011

Fifteen hours had passed and I finally had to ask, "Are you staying in bed because you are truly tired or are you staying in bed because you feel depressed?" The answer was tired. I knew too much sleep could make a person sleepier, but these weren't normal circumstances. Kel was experiencing two types of physical strains: flu-like symptoms involving pain and weakness or intoxication-type side effects (from the meds), which caused a loss in strength and coordination.

After I loudly voiced my concerns, he said, "I'm sure in a couple days I will feel better and then I will start the exercising."

There was such sadness in his eyes, and I believed his every word, but I looked at him and shouted, "We don't have a couple days! Over a week ago, the doctor told you these are crucial times!" Together, we busted through a wall, and for ten minutes we worked on his mobility.

With our warm clothes on, we were ready for a walk and the day. Kel was still dealing with facial numbness, so he wrapped his scarf around his head to prevent any possibility of frostbite. While walking, we met a woman and her dog. As our dogs sniffed, we introduced ourselves and she told us about her boyfriend's son, who owned a seeing-eye dog. The son lost his sight and arm in Iraq and was currently going through physical therapy. Things weren't going very well because he was struggling with the realities of his new life. We parted ways and I asked, "Kel, do you believe in coincidences?" After he said no, I felt the need to reiterate what had just happened. The story of a stranger's difficult recovery was close to home. It was home. Because we never disclosed or discussed Kelly's trials and tribulations, we felt honored this woman voluntarily shared with us something real and difficult. It had become clear the days were filled with inspiration and hope. Individuals were everywhere to help us grow, learn, and live.

## Sunday, March 27, 2011

Kel had one more treatment, and our thoughts were our own worst enemies. As the mind travels one hundred miles per minute, a tangled web of problems, what-ifs, and catastrophes have already been thought of. We needed to tell our minds, "Get back into reality, dumbass. Live in the now."

Kel and I processed information differently, which didn't make either of us wrong; it usually meant a discussion was brewing and created an opportunity to discover what made us tick or tock. During this particular circumstance, Kelly was forecasting his future fight against melanoma, and I tried to keep him in the present. It wasn't long ago I had a less than desirable image of my future and I had to learn to utilize thoughts and ideas that fueled my internal power and strength. A wise woman said, "Joe, why are you writing the pages of your life before they have been written?" I wasn't going to let anyone write my pages, and no matter what statistics Kel received, I wanted him to write his own. Stats, averages, and percentiles are based on several individual outcomes, but Kel was one person on his own path. If attitude was everything, Kel was going to be amazing. He accepted and dealt with his reality rather than denying and ignoring the truths. This was a survival skill we both had to learn before coming out.

Dealing with our sexuality gave us strength to face melanoma. Accepting and loving ourselves made acceptance of other circumstances possible. With any personal challenge comes obstacles, and Kel faced his every day. We had a lot of living left to do, and we were grateful for every moment we were granted.

## Monday, March 28, 2011

Before radiation, we met with a social worker. She told Kelly that acknowledging his inner questions and fears releases their control. Then she spoke the quote of the day: "Start doing life again." Live without fear. We were certainly making our best attempts.

For over one hour, patient after patient went by as I watched for Kel. Radiation was taking much longer than ever before, and butterflies filled my stomach until he rounded the corner with his mask in hand.

The bell did toll
If only in our head.

As we walk away
A new path we are led.

We are proud this chapter has been completed.
Our spirits, determination, and (inner) strength …
*undefeated!*

The road ahead we will walk together,
Believing (anything and everything) we can weather.

While Kel received his final treatment, I wrote and posted the above words on Caring Bridge. He had told me that he wasn't going to ring the bell, and it didn't matter because I knew it would ring in our minds.

We stepped through the parking ramp doors at the Mayo Clinic, and I said, "You are all done, Buck-A-Roo! Your last treatment is over." The moment I uttered those words, church bells in Rochester began to ring. They were so clear and solid. I told Kel they were ringing for him since he didn't ring the bell himself. He thought I was being silly, but I assured him this wasn't a coincidence. The bell ringing symbolized a new beginning, and I couldn't stop smiling ear to ear. It was the perfect end and a new beginning.

Before bed, I prescribed one peaceful night of dancing dreams, fantastic fantasies, and marvelous miracles. It was a gay dream!

# Chapter Four

## Recovery, Retesting, Restart

### Tuesday, March 29, 2011

Pill-popping had its challenges. Every drug had a different time schedule, and each pill turned into a razor blade ball as it hit Kel's throat. Every pill and swig of water went down with a hard swallow and a wince. Soft food choices (which consisted of sweet, sweeter, and sweetest) were less painful to swallow. *The privilege of existing* made any irritant tolerable.

Kel made time to exercise his wrist and neck. Full movement would make every aching stretch and bend worthwhile. I was proud he took the initiative. Throughout the day, his mood was stable and he completed a few light-duty chores. If he had any doubt of his capabilities, his accomplishments should have increased his confidence. March 29, 2011, was special. It only happened once, and I wanted Kelly to be proud of the day he had. March 30 was a reason to wake, live, and enjoy.

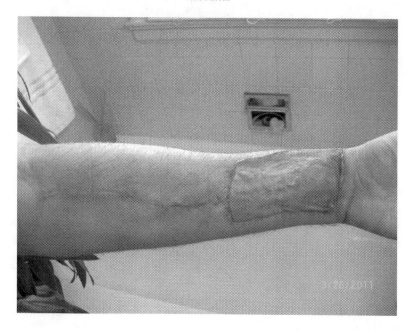

## Wednesday, March 30, 2011

My ears heard words that lifted the heart and soul of their owner. "Really, really good," was Kel's response when I asked about his day. He emitted enthusiasm and pride when he spoke those words. I was familiar with his silly side, the quiet side, the angry side, and the broken side, but this was a side of Kel I had not seen since prior to his surgery. I was unsure what the magic formula was other than the choices Kel had made. No matter how shitty we felt, there were choices that could make us feel better or worse.

Every day was a surprise, and every moment we were confronted with personal choices. Every choice would somehow alter future encounters, so we relied on our instincts and beliefs when deciding. All of my decisions were directly influenced by

Kelly's needs. I was neither obsessed nor consumed. Kel was an extension of my own being, and he deserved my undivided attention. My day was better and my heart was lighter because Kelly had a really good day. We weren't fighting against pill-popping, constant sleepiness, aches, and pains, because they were our inevitable reality; however, all other happenings and moments were choices we decided upon. We made the best of our choices and accomplished what we dared.

## Thursday, March 31, 2011

Highs and lows were expected on this roller coaster ride, but I continually wished for sunshine and roses. From the moment I woke, everything around me felt heavy. Even the morning conversation added to the heaviness. Yesterday, all the good emotions emerged, but on this day, the painful, annoying, exhausting ones surfaced. For months, Kelly had endured the scariest circumstances he had ever faced, and somehow he remained stable and strong. He proceeded with confidence and security. It was an awesome thing to witness and be part of. I tried to learn from his strengths.

His body and mind may have needed R & R, but Kel sought an activity he hoped would give him a sense of accomplishment: he cleaned his car. This was the first day since surgery that he washed his vehicle, and I believe it gave him a sense of pride. Through the kitchen window, I stared at him and wondered if he was overdoing it. I also felt a hint of jealousy that I wasn't getting as much attention as his car. I admired and respected Kelly for doing whatever he could to feel better and be happier.

**Kelly e-mailed this letter on the thirty-first:**

*Yesterday was good. I ventured out by myself (against doctor's orders because of all my prescriptions), but I just needed those couple hours of freedom. Needless to say, Joe wasn't happy until I pulled back into the garage. Please don't share my driving story with anyone as I wouldn't want them to think of me as a careless person. I understood the possible consequences when starting my car, but I just had to do it!*

# Friday, April 1, 2011

We had an appointment with a physical/occupational therapist at the Mayo Clinic. After examining Kelly's arm, the therapist informed us that Kel's graft had adhered to the tendons. In order to regain wrist mobility, several PT/OT sessions were needed to increase the fluid passing between the graft and tendons. Neck therapy was also recommended, which would help reduce swelling and promote minimal scarring. Kelly was told to concentrate on the therapeutic action or activity before it took place because it would promote a faster, more successful response within the area of focus.

I saw Kel's pain, I heard his words, but I couldn't feel or fix what he was going through. My writings were a biased depiction of his feelings and emotions, but I wasn't experiencing what he was going through. I continued to push and push because I thought I knew what was best for him, but I wasn't taking the time to hear what he needed. What Kel wanted or needed became my tightrope, and I wasn't sure if I was on the rope or freefalling. I didn't want to smother him, but that was exactly what happened. I knew what worked for me and that was what

I put forth, but I forgot to listen to what Kel's needs were and I tried to fix what I thought was broken.

Caring Bridge provided me an outlet through which to vent and verbalize the trials, tribulations, failures, and successes. Kelly didn't always love what I wrote, and I may have lacked a filter, but my intent was pure. Through my writing, I was attempting to emotionally unite us with our supporters in hopes of unifying our positive thoughts and creating a collective healing force for Kel.

Change can be greeted with resistance, frustration, and resentment but Kel's life had been turned upside down, inside out, and he accepted it, still able to smile and maintain a sense of humor. Kel's needs were drastically different from thirteen years prior, and I wanted to adapt and change to fulfill those needs. As our responsibilities shifted, our connection and love grew stronger.

## Saturday, April 2, 2011

Kel's benefit was two weeks away, which translated into fourteen days of progress, unpredictable circumstances, mood swings, random REM states, odd meal times, and no assumptions. These first twelve hours began with leftover frustrations from the previous day. We agreed to separately experience the same sunny, beautiful day in ways that fit our wants and needs. Kel had breakfast with his family, but his mouth ulcers affected any enjoyable moment that once accompanied eating or drinking. With every passing hour, talking was becoming more painful.

I became aware that I was consumed with Kel's well-being more than my own, and that often caused tension between us. I had to learn how to trust his decisions even if I didn't agree with them. I had to believe he was doing everything he could for his recovery even if I wanted him to do more. I had my own life to control, and Kel certainly didn't want me to run his. Pull apart and come together, pull apart and come together—every challenge had a solution. Several learning curves came with cancer, but I was confident we'd come out on top. By nightfall, we quietly reconnected.

## Sunday, April 3, 2011

We knew the worst radiation side effects could take place one week after the final treatment. They did. Stomach cramps and mouth ulcers were taking their toll. As the ulcers shed, Kel removed the chunks of dead skin from his mouth. There wasn't anything he was expecting; he just wanted to feel better.

The words, "At least you're through the worst part," seemed relative. Optimistic catchphrases were often said in an attempt to make Kel feel better or to offer us comfort. I used them but not as often as we heard them, and I wondered if Kelly was tired of hearing these inspiring quotes. I could have asked but I thought he would sarcastically say, "Why are you asking? Do you need something to write about?"

It took me a long time to acknowledge Kel needed moments to forget about cancer. Unfortunately, pain was a constant internal reminder, and I was the external reminder. While Kel was permanently in combat with cancer, I was trying to find new methods he could use to fight. I should have stopped doing what I thought was right and asked myself who it was right for. I was blinded by my desire to save him.

## Monday, April 4, 2011

Incapacitated and completely miserable—that's what I saw when I looked at Kel. I couldn't tell how intense his pain was, but the only place he appeared somewhat comfortable was in bed. I wondered if he had irritable bowels, because his hunched-over stature and pain replicated my own experiences. There had been little sign of Kel's uplifting spirit, and I was praying for relief. Little time was spent communicating, and I did my best to comfort from afar.

## Tuesday, April 5, 2011

The unanimous suggested pain reliever from our peers was a hot bath. The water was running, Kel was resting comfortably, and Chaos decided to jump in and join his daddy in the tub. The bath may have been good for the pain, but Chaos was good for his heart and soul. A thirty-minute soak together may have caused pruning, but it also helped remove the fog that masked Kel's spirit.

I remembered days when there was no concern of any kind, and I yearned for an hour or two when our minds were clear of any cancerous thoughts. Instead, we were seeing the cause and effect every day. Kel had just gotten out of the tub and said, "Want a gift?" I declined as he pulled dead skin from his mouth ulcers and extended it toward me. I was happy that, once again, he was able to make light out of an unfunny situation.

We received a list of all of the possible side effects, but my heart broke in two when Kel rubbed his face and his hands became covered in whiskers. I burst into tears after he went to bed because I didn't want him to see my pain. We had reached the beginning of another phase, and neither of us could deny or change it. While supporting one another, we took time to process separately. We couldn't change what was, so we did our best to accept it and move forward.

## Wednesday, April 6, 2011

During my morning drive, I was listening to Out Q radio and the deejays discussed ways in which people cope (or not) with emotional crisis. I was still processing my reaction to the whiskers, but this quote caught my ears: "Bad times come to pass, but they don't come to stay." That statement had great perspective and helped me surpass my immediate hang-ups.

In case Kel was sleeping, I limited my check-in calls. When I did reach him, he was washing the dishes, and I know I smiled. I knew he must have been feeling better. By the time I got home, the house was clean and he was resting. We chatted about our day, and before he could resist, we were out walking with Chaos.

Kel's stomach was still uneasy, but it was a functional queasy. He wasn't at 100 percent, but compared to previous days, he was looking like a million bucks. It was a cloudy sky above our home, but the sun was shining inside.

Every tomorrow was like a Cracker Jack box. We could try to predict what awaited us—sometimes a thrill, sometimes a buzz kill—but we were always full of hope.

## Saturday, April 9, 2011

We had different schedules, abilities, expectations, and challenges; we coexisted, but not always on a parallel plane. I was feeling I could do no right, and I wasn't feeling grounded. Kel couldn't heal fast enough, and his patience and perseverance seemed nonexistent. I tried to duck and dodge Kelly's abrasive button-pushing tactics, but the sharpness of his tongue got my blood boiling. We were both strong-minded, and disagreements came with solo opinions and loud voices—mostly mine. Arguments had always been building blocks for our relationship, but Kel wasn't typically the instigator (I realized just how annoying an instigator can be) and I wanted that position back. Being emotionally close to another person definitely influenced and altered our state of mind and behavior.

When Kel was feeling better and we readjusted into cohesive living, I was writing in Caring Bridge and asked Kel if he had anything to add. He said, "Tell them it was a horrible week. I had two hours a day of energy, if that. My stomach has been awful, and I haven't really eaten. But today was a good day." Based on what he said, I knew he wasn't grounded either, but we were reestablishing our footing.

## Sunday, April 10, 2011

Kel's throat was giving him little trouble and he ate more this day than he had the previous three, but he said the food tasted like shit. Facial swelling had gone down, and all other areas of concern were healing nicely. His right lobe was regaining some feeling, but the sensation from touch felt icky. Kelly's stomach had settled, and his mood stabilized. Our home was filled with imaginary visions of smiley faces and happy hearts.

## Tuesday, April 12, 2011

Melanoma was a hard blow, and Kelly's sparkle and zest for life weren't as shiny and bright as they normally were. His plate had been overflowing for months, and I wondered how he was coping emotionally, mentally, and physically. It would have been easy to assume everything was moving along perfectly, especially when I witnessed Kel's increased progress, but lurking in the dark was fear that cancer had returned. In one day, Kel was going to have his follow-up scans, and there wasn't a pep talk or prepping that could eliminate the anxiety. We prayed for the perfect scenario, and that gave us hope, but it still didn't give us a solid result.

What Kel had experienced, I could deem too difficult to go through, but he had no other option. Healing was not simple or quick, and despite his fear, Kel maintained an optimistic attitude. Each time we discussed a fear, we dismantled its grasp and gained positivity and control.

## Wednesday, April 13, 2011

A scale at the Mayo Clinic proved what I could see: Kel had definitely lost weight. Maintaining weight and hydration had been challenging because everything tasted awful, every swallow was painful, and he always felt full. Kelly told me it was difficult getting food or liquid down his throat because it sat there, as if his stomach had a cap on it. In order to have his cancer tests done, Kelly had to drink (force) several liquids, and during that time, many of his cramping, painful issues mellowed. I strongly believed (and every document suggested) water was a major source for decreasing side effects. Kel didn't believe in charting his food or liquid intake, but it could have shown us if certain foods and drinks affected his pain levels.

I have witnessed individuals making dietary choices that could worsen their situations, even though they were aware of their health conditions. I have never understood why anyone would consciously make a choice that could potentially harm them. Kel didn't choose cancer, but I did want him to intentionally choose things that would help his fight against it. Control of his food and drink intake may have seemed like the easiest way for him to assist his fight, but he was accustomed to eating whatever he wanted, whenever he wanted. Healthy choices had always been within reach, but it was difficult to retrain the mind and body connection to food. Years ago, I began asking myself, "How is this going to fuel my body?" I was hoping Kelly would adapt to that way of thinking, because he had an internal battle to end.

"When am I going to wake up from this nightmare?" Kel said as he looked for answers within my sadness. The PET scan exposed trouble spots on his rib, bottom of his chest, upper abdomen, mid liver, spine, and pelvis. There was major concern, and a biopsy was scheduled to determine if his melanoma had spread. We were assured by a surgeon we had options, alternatives, and hope, and they would figure out the best way to treat Kel.

It was impossible for us to get our minds wrapped around what we had heard. How could we? Kel's only focus should have been his health, but he began to worry about his car, job, and bills. I was experiencing a crushed spirit, heartache, worry, fear, and sadness. Kel and I went back to our hotel room, called our families, held one another, and cried ourselves to sleep. Only sleep reduced these pains.

Awake with clear minds, we both said, "Well, it is what it is, and now we go forward." Kel and I spent the evening sharing laughter, joy, and flashbacks of our time together.

Until Kelly was 100 percent healthy, my love for him could not be expressed enough or shined upon him enough to satisfy my need to do so. I knew my focus and attention would drive him crazy and we would both yearn for the days when our ignorance was bliss. We needed to live every moment and absorb the positivity. Each day was a gift and our lives had a purpose, as did everything that happened throughout.

## Thursday, April 14, 2011

In some ways, I felt like we were right at the beginning (same feelings, same emotions, same fight), and yet the fighting spirit was stronger than ever. Before leaving the hospital on Wednesday, we had to book another hotel room, so we used that "pick your price and get a good deal" site. We ended up in a hotel directly across the street from where Kel's biopsy was taking place. Funny how a random purchase didn't feel random at all and the wonders continued to surround us.

Waiting was really a horrible thing, and sitting alone was not good for me. During the first hour, I couldn't stop my tears, and all of my tissues were sopping. Thank God I wasn't a makeup wearer because that shit would have streaked down my face. I spoke with my sister, and she told me to think the way I want life to be. Isn't that what I did as a kid? When did life become harder to deal with? I was supposed to be older and wiser.

The biopsy took over four hours, and they removed three tissue samples from his liver. They went through his stomach with a needle to retrieve these samples, and Kel experienced after-pains. For twenty-four hours, we were required to watch for any troubling signs or complications from the biopsy. There were none.

On our drive home, we made several stops, and it felt like life as usual. The drive gave us ample time to chat about many topics, and it also induced tears and laughter. We had our first conversation about our mortality, and Kel wanted to make sure that if he lost his battle, I would be taken care of. Since we were gay, and out of concern for my protection, Kel wanted to switch everything into my name. I denied his request, because life was a mystery without a guarantee that I would live longer than him. Being with Kelly made me happy and I wasn't ready to think about life any differently, so we agreed to discuss the topic at a later date. We drove on, knowing cancer and our fears needed to be hip-checked out of our lives, like an unworthy opponent.

Our arrival home looked like a scene after one of our vacations—Kel was sprawled out on the couch while I unpacked and did the laundry. Our life was a game in many ways: we played hard, got tired, rested, and regrouped for the next challenge. Kel's benefit was in two days, and we planned on celebrating our victories. He was a survivor, still fighting.

## Friday, April 15, 2011

A phone call from the Mayo Clinic confirmed it was melanoma.

I wanted an action plan, and Kel needed time to process. It was impossible to know or understand what Kelly was going through, and the more I tried to get inside, the more he shut me out. I wasn't very good at just listening because I always wanted to make it better or fix it. I now know that I needed to trust and believe in Kel because he wanted to be better.

There was no chance of surgically removing all of the cancerous areas; therefore, chemotherapy was advised. Doctors had to complete a detailed study of both Kel's DNA and the melanoma before deciding on the best chemo options. Kel had two weeks to get stronger and healthier while those studies took place.

## Saturday, April 16, 2011

Love can conquer all, and we were going to wipe cancer from Kel's body, but we didn't know how long it would take or how much pain he'd have to endure. Kelly was exhausted from the pain, meds, and emotions, and he felt much like he did after his surgery. When he laughed, cried, coughed, sneezed, talked, and inhaled deeply, it hurt, but nothing was going to stop Kel from making an appearance at his benefit. Surrounding Kelly with love and support was the perfect way to boost morale.

Every day I was told inspiring stories that lifted my spirits, but Kel didn't have the opportunity to hear these truths, and I wondered if they would help at all. Uplifting stories can invoke a belief that anything is possible and miracles do happen, but I was fully aware the path ahead was Kelly's alone. My support was all I had to offer, and it wasn't able to give him the comfort I wanted it to. Kel wanted to feel better, and time held the power. Two months had passed, and this reality still wasn't making sense, but the unification of our loved ones was a miracle in itself.

## Sunday, April 17, 2011

I never want to live a life that no longer surprises me, a life unable to offer me experiences that put me in awe, or a life without family and friends.

The benefit was everything. Kel and I shared many sobbing moments that represented the richness we felt. I was never monetarily rich and I didn't need to be, because events like the benefit made me aware of the riches I had.

Though I tried to resist, I had expectations. I wanted the benefit to overflow Kel's capability of taking it all in, and it ended up overflowing mine as well. It was phenomenal in every way, shape, and form. Kel and I cherished every party we attended because each was a unique celebration of whatever we wanted it to be. Life is a party, or at least it should be. The benefit was our first party since melanoma arrived, and we may have looked exhausted but we had never been more alive. The light within Kel shined bright as he lived in the presence of time. His spirits and emotions were lifted to a new high. At one point, I walked outside and the only blue sky was directly above. It didn't last long, but I believed it gave passage for all of the love and support from beyond. It was priceless.

I never want to live a life that no longer surprises me, a life unable to offer me experiences that put me in awe, or a life without family and friends.

**Kel shared this experience with me; interpret it how you will:**

I was asleep at 3:30 a.m., and Kel was next to me. Every time he shut his eyes during the next two and a half hours, he experienced a steady stream of unrecognizable people with smiling faces, clear eyes, and open arms coming toward him for a hug. It made him kind of dizzy and nauseous because it was happening so fast. It also freaked him out, and he said he almost woke me up. When he would open his eyes, they would disappear, but the stream of individuals continued the moment he would close them. The situation didn't make him feel unsafe, and they were never able to physically give him a hug, but their presence was known. Everyone was standing and chatting in a line, waiting to see Kel, and after each approached, he saw them walk away. The vividness of their eyes, mouths, eyebrows, and arms made him believe this was what being welcomed into heaven would be like.

## Monday, April 18, 2011

Many of the moments I shared with Kel were taken for granted, but it seemed like there would be time to appreciate things at a later date. It had been thirteen years since we met, and I didn't know where the heck that time went, but I did know how fortunate I was to be by his side. I wasn't sure if straight people had a different term to coin other strong, happy, established couples, but Kel and I had often been called a power couple. I don't think many individuals or couples view themselves the way others do, but when Kel was by my side, I always felt powerful. He brought out the best in me, and all I wanted to do was spend more time with him.

I started to think I needed chanting cheerleaders in my ears so my mind stayed current and my thoughts were unable to drift. When I drifted, I shifted my focus to "fight, fight, fight, fight," and I used my telepathetic (telepathic and pathetic) powers to send this message to Kel. I felt better, and it kept me in the present, but the best feelings came when I spoke with Kel.

I loved hearing Kel say, "I feel good," and he had felt this way for three days. His energy was better, he was doing his PT/OT exercises, and he was sleeping more soundly. Kel's life, like every life, could be summed up by chapters. It would have been wrong for cancer to take the lead as we wrote these chapters because Kel was the main character: strong, obstinate, fun, honest, open, kind, loving, and the one I loved. Cancer sucked and it wasn't worth our time to dwell on it. I had given the lead to cancer a few times and that had to stop because it didn't even deserve a supporting role. I lived a good portion of life denying myself because fear led me. When I accepted the situation, control became mine and life was full of possibility.

## Tuesday, April 19, 2011

Kel's eyes were bright and his laughter roared through the house. His appetite was getting better every day, and it seemed like time did heal all wounds. Two weeks to process and prepare, heal and get stronger, absorb the positive energy, and build morale while living and loving life. It felt like a gift. We were walking with Chaos, and as I looked at him, I asked myself, "What's wrong with him?" It was a day of sharing, laughing, and enjoying.

Kel's appearance was once a huge priority, but he admitted that he was content and owning his scars. He had been avoiding short sleeves because of the arm graft, but he informed me that he was going to wear the scars with pride and he hoped people would ask what happened. Kelly wanted to share his story and potentially inspire others who may have had a similar experience. I felt his determination, desire, and overall passion when he looked at me and said, "I want to live!" His conviction nearly brought him to tears as my respect and pride for him overflowed.

## Wednesday, April 20, 2011

Kel had twenty-four hours a day to focus solely on himself, but it was nothing less than a full-time job. Duties, tasks, and mental and medical audits were performed daily. Weight gain was a goal, balancing medical invoices was a must, exercise was a choice, and relaxation resulted in sleeping or wrapping his thoughts around what he had accomplished or needed to accomplish.

After two and a half months, I finally understood that what I trusted and believed offered me the best chance of personal advancement and achievement. What worked for me could be completely different from what Kel felt would work for him. Throughout our lives, we built upon those trusts and beliefs; there was no right or wrong. I wanted Kel to trust and believe in (some) things like I did. Regardless, he always deserved my support for his every decision. My eyes watched my words get written, but it took time to incorporate the lesson learned.

## Thursday, April 21, 2011

Caring Bridge entry:

*Hey everyone, it's me again, Kelly. I know Joe has already elaborated on our thoughts and feelings regarding the benefit, so please forgive me if my words sound familiar, but I have to express this for myself.*

*Wow... where to start?*

*I arrived at the VFW around 2:40 p.m. with absolutely no expectations. Entering the building, I immediately felt like a celebrity. All eyes focused on me, and everyone was smiling. From that moment, I knew it was going to be a night like nothing I had ever experienced.*

*So about thirty feet in (the VFW) and thirty minutes later, I needed to take my first break and sit for a few. At this point I was able to focus on everything that was going on all around me. Elvis (Ken Sutherland) was performing and everyone was really enjoying him. From there, I looked toward the dance floor, which was converted to a well set-up silent auction area. Soon announcements were being made about raffles, chance boards, etc., and friends were off and running, selling tickets left and right. Needless to say, what I was witnessing was hard work all being put forth for one person: me. With emotions now running high, I remember talking to myself, stating,* Stay strong and hold it together. *It seemed to work for a bit but not all night. I guess what I'm trying to get at is, this was a very special night for me, Joe, and my family, and there are no words to describe my gratitude toward the group of individuals who helped make this possible.* Thank you! Thank you! Thank you!

*As for now, I'm patiently waiting for the Mayo to call so I can start my next set of treatments. I'm keeping positive, and this includes joking regularly. One thing I have joked about is that I will be fine losing my hair on my head, but if my eyebrows disappear, I may just have to draw them in.*

*"Maybe he was born with it … Maybe it's Gay-beline!"*

# Friday, April 22, 2011

While we walked with Chaos, Kel's words were spoken with sad inflections as he talked about the weekend and what we would normally be doing. I think reflections from the benefit party were making him thirsty for more excitement. Priorities changed to coincide with Kel's health, and I began to question if our old weekend habits were more of a rut than a routine.

*Exciting* no longer defined our weekends ... *responsible* did. Kelly finally attacked all of his medical bills and wrote thousands of dollars in checks. I was paging through a monthly periodical and came across an article that brought forth familiar emotions and confirmed everything we knew. Melanoma was a crazy, unthinkable intruder in our lives and it was impossible not to be afraid. Embracing life in the now had its challenges.

I believed the way our body and mind functioned was directly impacted by how we treated it. I had to believe that melanoma could be defeated using the same sort of philosophy. Success relied on Kel and what he believed would work for him. I hoped he wasn't underestimating his own mental and physical power over it. If he felt helpless, it was an injustice to him because there was an abundance of love and support surrounding him. Wish it true, think it true, believe it true, and make it true.

# Saturday, April 23, 2011

The sheets and mattress pad were soaked with sweat, and Kel's entire body was achy and exhausted. His temp was normal, but he looked like he would have a 103 degree reading. I wasn't sure if the cancer was releasing toxins or if Kel's body was defending what was rightfully his. Kelly felt better after the sweating stopped, but it took a lot out of him, and sleep, along with fluids, were his rejuvenators. While he slept, it felt natural to comfort—but not wake—him in hopes of transferring positivity into his dream sequence.

## Sunday, April 24, 2011

As we got closer to my parent's home, my heart smiled and then giggled. Easter was a time of new beginnings, and this particular Easter had a new first. Our families lived one hundred and twenty miles apart, and for twelve years we went our separate ways, but this year we brought everyone together. Approximately thirty-five people shared the day and created incredible memories.

Kelly and I were fortunate to have similar, awesome family backbones. In the gay community, it was rare to have parents who loved not only us, but also one another. With a lump in my throat and tears falling from my eyes, I acknowledged how incredibly rich we were. Shedding a tear for our fortunes made me feel as if I knew what being alive was all about. Kel and I retired for the night with our hearts inspired and bursting with love. Our first Easter together was lived in the present but would be part of us forever and ever.

# Chapter Five

## Equal Parts Tears and Laughter

### Monday, April 25, 2011

At 5:45 a.m., pain magnitude was ten out of ten. "There is something really wrong. I need to go to the ER," Kel cried out as he woke me. A CAT scan ruled out a collapsed lung, blood clot, or a pulled muscle, but it revealed that the cancer had spread and grown. A tumor pressed between Kel's lung and ribcage was the culprit. The scan also showed that his left fourth rib was cracked from a different tumor.

Even though Kelly's DNA tests (for treatment options) were still pending, the Mayo doctor felt it was necessary to begin chemo before the end of the week. We made open-ended travel arrangements and packed for an extended stay in Rochester. Kel's family came to our home to wish him well, and they were welcomed with his smartass humor and optimism. Kelly was definitely the driver, but we were all there to help him steer.

My faith and hope had not been swayed, but I was scared and worried. I planned to be by Kel's side each step of the way, offering every ounce of love I had. Watching and hearing his anguish affected me most and was the source of my helpless feelings. Kel realized I was having a difficult time with his new diagnosis, and he held me and said, "I'm going to beat this, Joe, and after all this shit is over, we will get back to our normal lives!" I was holding on to his words, and once again, my heart smiled.

The demons of the past had been fought, and here we were, ready for more. Buffy the Vampire Slayer kicked demons' asses, and I wanted to be Kelly's slayer and kick the shit out of melanoma or anything that hurt him. On many occasions, Kel had said, "Well, what choice do I have?" He made the choice to fight and kick the shit out of his demons because he wanted to live.

## Tuesday, April 26, 2011

Fear was life-altering; it either controlled us or we controlled it. Because of cancer, Kel and I had individual and shared fear, but that also helped us grow. During Kel's Mayo Clinic appointment, our optimism wasn't swayed by the stats put forth because we knew others had beaten the odds. Facts may have initially scared us but we heard them, processed them, and then moved forward with a plan. We may not have had the power to create the perfect outcome, but we had proven bonding together created an invincible force of love.

Question: When are you considered a cancer survivor?
Answer: The day you are diagnosed!

*Live large.*

## Wednesday, April 27, 2011

Test, test, test … was this really happening? Kel and I needed to have adult conversations that still seemed too adult to have, and the topics felt like they were getting more difficult to face. I was forced to acknowledge how life had changed, and it made me a bit crazed and insane. I never thought ordinary would be something I would desire, but it became all I craved. After having a brief personal breakdown, it became clear I was trying to welcome in as much emotion as I was releasing—equal parts tears and laughter. Our tears may have flourished, but Kel and I lived, and lived well, in laughter. Life was full of incredible things, within our grasp and ours for the taking. We were coming for them.

## Thursday, April 28, 2011

Chemo was used to shrink tumors and potentially extend, but not save, the life of melanoma patients. There was not a medical cure. An MRI proved Kel's brain was clear of melanoma and therefore he was accepted into a clinical study that incorporated a new drug that had shown promising effects in some patients. Doctors said without chemo, Kel could expect to live six to seven more months, but with chemo, his life expectancy increased to twelve to fifteen months. Less than 5 percent of melanoma patients had survived, and they did so without chemo or radiation. They were the miracles. Very few facts were known about the 5 percent because their successes were achieved outside of the documented medical practice. I was intrigued and encouraged by the 5 percent, but I believed and supported Kel's decision to have chemo. I respected Kelly and what he thought would be his success.

Kel had continuously said, "Cancer is not who I am. I will not allow melanoma to upset my family and friends, and I am going back to work." I believed him. He was on a personal journey to discover and navigate a healing energy.

## Friday, April 29, 2011

Twenty-four hours after chemo, the sun was shining bright, and morale-lifting conversations filled us with happiness and freed us from cancer. I cherished the moments when melanoma wasn't part of my thoughts or way of life, and I was sure Kel felt the same.

We took a family stroll along Lake Superior, and Kel sat behind a boulder near the shore, to shield him from the wind. While he absorbed some rays, Chaos ran wild and tried to get gulps of lake water. I watched as small waves crashed upon the rocks; the splashes made him scamper. I enjoyed the sights, especially watching Kel relax and absorb every ounce of beauty that had been lost upon us in the past. I grabbed a seat next to Kel, and together we were free. He told me to give him a kiss and said, "If people want to hurt us because we're gay, I will just say, do you want a piece of this cancer? Huh, do ya?" We kissed—our first kiss at Lake Superior's shore! That was real, that was living free. We were in love.

## Saturday, April 30, 2011

Chemo side effects had been exactly how I had imagined: minimal. Kel did wake with a headache, which lasted much of the day, and I was dealing with my own annoyances.

There was concern I wasn't taking time for myself, and many (unwanted) advisers told me I should take a few days to get away from the situation. Several people may have felt I needed a mental break, but they were also relying on me to be their messenger. It was a double-edged sword: concern for my mental health, while piling more on my plate. Kel was already being doused with my overbearing, overprotective, overloving self, and I wasn't about to overwhelm him with medical opinions others wanted me to share. Nor was I going to step away for any amount of time.

While Kel slept through the day, memories from our past played in my head. Songs took me back, as if they had a time-stamp on them. Everything about the day made me aware of who I was and how I got here: my own personal reflection created by every emotion of my past. There were many tears that Kel was able to avoid and I was able to freely release.

## Sunday, May 1, 2011

I forewarned Kelly that if he wanted to avoid my constant nagging, there were three things I needed him to do: eat, exercise, and drink plenty of fluids. Sweet foods were the core of Kel's diet, but the clinical study chemo drug had potential side effects that required him to eliminate fatty foods, and this added to his eating challenge. Exercise routines were supplied through therapy, and our daily family walks kept us moving. Liquid intake was going well, but the taste became the biggest obstacle to overcome.

## Monday, May 2, 2011

I had a difficult time imagining a moment of mental silence because I was mulling continually. I was questioning everything as I tried to predict or analyze causes and effects. I was seeking perfection, and the impossibility of that felt miserable. My impatience and expectations should have been checked at the door, but I couldn't stop fighting for Kel's health. Every day we were being educated and moving forward, I just had to believe we were doing everything as best we could. It was difficult, and I had to tell myself, "Just breathe."

## Tuesday, May 3, 2011

The moment I heard Kel's voice, I knew it was going to be an absolutely wonderful day. I felt empowered when Kel was empowered, and he sounded strong. We weren't cohesive in the previous days, but we reunited and continued our fight against the common enemy: melanoma. This day became one that I wanted future days to mimic.

Kel topped the two thousand calorie mark and I was so proud of this accomplishment. Fatigue was present, but he went on three separate walks while taking advantage of the weather. He opened up and shared his thoughts, and I saw the fight and desire I wanted (and needed). I also learned he was worried about my welfare; he disliked our lack of normalcy, and his inability to physically function the way he wanted weighed heavily on him. Our home life had rocky moments, but communication remained at the core and carried us through.

Every time I left the house, I couldn't wait to come back home and see Kel. I had lost myself in a previous relationship, but I found myself in this one. Kel's candle burned brightly within and it made mine shine brighter.

## Wednesday, May 4, 2011

In order for me to accompany Kel to his Mayo Clinic treatments, my work schedule was constantly adjusted. After I worked my day shift, we took Chaos for a very long walk and enjoyed the summer weather. Back at home, I was very tired, so I grabbed my pillow, placed it on Kel's lap, and slept like a baby. Upon waking, I gathered my bearings and Kel went to the kitchen to wash the dishes and clean the fish aquarium. His energy and stamina filled me with happiness and peace. I wanted to continue watching him but I had another shift of work. When I got home, Kelly informed me that he wrote on Caring Bridge so I didn't have to.

**Kelly's CB entries were few, but they always conveyed love.**

*Hey everyone, Kelly here,*
*Tonight's journal entry is being dedicated to my other family, the Petersons.*

*What to say about a family that is so close-knit and yet always has room in their hearts for others? Well let's just say my vocabulary isn't expanded enough to try to attempt it, and I refuse to ask Joe to write this for me.*

*What I can say:*

*1)* Thank you *for welcoming me into your family!*
*2)* Thank you *for teaching me the power behind the words* I love you!
*3)* Thank you *for all the memories!*
*And last but certainly not least,*
*4)* Thank you *for Joe!*

*I love you all very much and couldn't imagine my life without you!*

*With that said, get used to me being around because I'm not going anywhere for many, many years!*

**Kelly also sent this email on May fourth:**

*As I sit here enjoying my iced coffee, I'm reflecting on how lucky I am to have stumbled across such a wonderful and loving family! Not only did I end up with a wonderful partner, but I most definitely* hit the jackpot *when it came to all of you. Thanks so much for making my journey easier to stomach.*

# Thursday, May 5, 2011

Round two of chemo was also an opportunity to gain information and fine-tune our at-home efforts. Everything that was suggested, Kel had already been doing: a two-thousand calorie diet, daily walks, and naps. Kelly was being proactive, and it was time for chemo to assist his inner-determination in destroying the intruder. I sat with Kel as he received a bag of liquid Benadryl. Next to him sat an empty pretzel bag, and he started to say, "Those really dried out my mou—" His eyes were partly closed when he began the sentence, and halfway through his statement, his eyes darted side to side while his mouth fell open like a fish. He was out like a light, and all I could do was laugh.

While Kel slept, my eyes studied the fifty-, sixty-, and seventy-year-olds who were receiving chemo and fighting for their right to live. I imagined each of them looked at Kel and sadly thought, "So young." Unlike our society, cancer wasn't prejudiced.

## Friday, May 6, 2011

On February 12, 2011, friends offered to purchase us two tickets for an upcoming Elton John concert. We obviously said yes! We knew Kel had melanoma but were unaware of the travels on which we'd embark. After every devastating blow to our morale, Kel questioned if we should sell our tickets. He even told me to have a back-up plan so I wouldn't end up going alone. My expression could have translated into, "Are you fucking kidding me?" Almost three months later, we were among several queens waiting to see Elton.

I watched couples (defined by closed-minded individuals as a man and a woman) hold one another in a loving embrace. I learned something about a limitation I had. Touch was used to encourage, love, guide, comfort, and hold, but Kel and I never felt safe to touch in public. I didn't feel safe saying what I was feeling because I didn't trust my surroundings to be free of hate. In public, Kel never felt my hugs when my love for him overwhelmed me, and he never heard me say, "I love you," as often as I would have liked. It was after our first gay cruise when we became conscious of real life and how much we catered to societal prejudices. We altered our actions in order to be safe, to feel safe. Because Elton John was gay, I felt less fear showing Kel some public affection, and I wrapped my arm around him. The bass from every song travelled through our entire being, and I envisioned every boom demolishing the tumors in Kel's body. I listened more openly, heard much more meaning, and lived Out with Kel.

"And you can tell everybody, this is your song. I hope you don't mind, I hope you don't mind that I put down in words … how wonderful life is while you're in the world!" As Elton began his last song, "Your Song," we all stood. I knew the words but never grasped them. During this final performance, Kel held my hand, my eyes welled up, and I thought, *How wonderful my life is with Kel in my world.*

The lights came on and as we headed for the exit door, Kel grabbed my hand and pulled it close. I was proud of his initiative but I became concerned over negative reactions and feared possible hateful encounters. I held his hand tighter as I wondered how long he would hold my hand and speculated our point of letting go. Our grasp was released at the exit doors, but reunited as we walked to the car. Unfortunately, our consciousness of society accompanied our first public hand-hold.

## Sunday, May 8, 2011

It was Mother's Day, and our lives began there. Kel spent the day with his mom and I traveled to be with mine. Our mothers always allowed for our mistakes and accepted our truths. They made us feel special and loved.

## Monday, May 9, 2011

Kelly had his most enjoyable and active weekend since January, and today he felt like someone punched him in the gut. A previous scan had exposed a cancerous spot on his stomach, and I wondered if it was flaring up. I found myself wishing Kel's reality untrue, but that only brought the depth of scariness to the forefront. What was it going to take to rid this poison from his body? I felt mentally handcuffed as my mind aimlessly searched for answers.

It felt like we were chasing balance and harmony, and when we would catch it, we struggled to keep it. Maintained balance and harmony: goodness can't defy it and all that is evil will succumb to it.

## Tuesday, May 10, 2011

Stomach issues persisted, but Kel made a conscious statement when he said, "It's going to be a good day." Kel's honed communication skills and mastered personal relations were his strengths at work, and he utilized them when he spent the day discussing his return and catching up with coworkers. After his socializing, Kel had intentions of returning home and taking a nap, but his mouth would not quiet.

Everyone who knew Kel was affected by his melanoma. Kelly seemed to know the only way he could expand his inner self was by allowing outside resources in. His personal growth and truth was inspired by all.

## Wednesday, May 11, 2011

**Kelly sent this e-mail to a friend:**

*Howdy! Been sick the last couple of days and have a couple of sores in my mouth that make speaking unpleasant. Chemo tomorrow (Thursday), and I'm finally starting to feel better, which will make the car ride much easier. Got some excellent news from my work, and they will wait for me as long as it takes. I told them I hope to return within a month. They are also fine with me coming back and slowly working back into full-time. Unfortunately, I'm now on zero pay and I needed to purchase one month of Cobra insurance at $1,062 (ouch). This alone will make the push for me to return full-time. All I can say is thank God for the benefit!*

## Thursday, May 12, 2011

The first chemo drug of the day was flowing, and I sat quietly, questioning, "What have I learned, what have I gained, have I been good enough, and how can I be better?" I wanted answers that would make us feel better and a promise that would solidify our security. I knew my only healthy option was to trust Kel's decisions and follow his lead, but it was difficult for me to be a follower. We were stubborn individuals who assisted the personal growth of each other.

We finally had that conversation about mortality. Kel shared his wishes, and I was able to listen without denial. Kelly admitted he had been trying to shelter me from anguish, and I acknowledged my obsession with his health. Even after thirteen years, there were many things to accept about one another, but communication, love, and understanding already built something pretty awesome and amazing. My love for Kel may have made me feel out of control, but I had never felt more complete.

## Friday, May 13, 2011

It felt like a blink of an eye ago our lives were in a scrambler. The road ahead seemed difficult to venture, and there was no return to the road traveled. After months of forging through, things felt as if they were settling; Kel had finished his third chemo treatment, and side effects were minimal. Therapy helped increase his wrist mobility by 30 percent, and the graft edges were finally flush with his arm. The flap had blended with the surrounding facial tissue, and feeling was returning. Kel's leg had healthy-colored flesh emerging through the fading purplish memory.

At my request, we made a list to help maintain focus and direction. "Free Kel's body, soul, and spirit from melanoma, tumors, and pain. Increase Kel's white blood cells to protect him from invisible turmoil. Kel's PET, MRI, and CAT scans will be clean, clear, and normal. Keep hair!" Kel requested "Keep hair" be added to the list, and I thought it was sweet but vulnerable. This list was placed on Caring Bridge so other prayers and wishes would unite with our objectives. We were forging ahead and building support.

## Saturday, May 14, 2011

One of the oddest statements was said by several individuals: "Start creating as many memories as you can." Didn't every living moment become a memory and, therefore, special in its own right? Our entire existence was a sum of our memories, and we were still adding on. We didn't need to start creating memories, because living our lives made them happen naturally.

As we walked with Chaos, our pace was much slower than usual. When Kel and I rested on the side of a hill, the most spectacular thing happened. We shared our childhood struggles, hatred we encountered, and how being gay affected us. Kel admitted that he had never shared these memories because he didn't want to relive the pain. His candor confirmed that our childhood experiences were very similar and painful. Sharing our stories freed us from our childhood turmoil and brought us closer together. We lived an uncalculated, unexpected, unplanned, and unforced moment. Now, it's a special *memory*.

## Sunday, May 15, 2011

Kel woke with some chest pain, and I went to work with his discomfort on my mind. It wasn't the way I wanted to start a new week, so I didn't. I said some affirmations and made the choice to have a good day. Kel felt the presence of pain, but only he had control over his day, so when I arrived home, we made more affirmations.

I witnessed Kel's personal growth, and it was an incredibly humbling process for me. I wasn't sure if he was aware of how much he had adapted to change, sought after answers, and accepted his journey. Every moment may have seemed like a continuum that he moved with, but he was in control. I wondered how I would handle what Kel had endured, and

I hoped I could exude the confidence, security, and honor he had.

Chemo wasn't scheduled for the week, but Kel still had follow-up appointments at the Mayo Clinic, making car travel inevitable. The radio was off the entire time, and we talked nonstop. Our conversations had a depth Kel used to avoid, and I felt our connection deepen. What remained a key factor in our partnered success was our ability to grow together. Today we bloomed. The night was for rest, and tomorrow was our canvas.

## Monday, May 16, 2011

I've learned that eyes can deceive what hands can feel. The surgeon closed his eyes as he felt around Kel's neck and flap, and then reported there weren't any signs of melanoma. I breathed and then asked if there were any foods proven beneficial to cancer patients. According to him, exercise, rest, and a plant-based diet have all been proven to assist the fight. Kel verbalized his dislike of most fruits and veggies and was told to enjoy life first and foremost. The surgeon ended with "I have *no* reason to believe that you won't be around for many years to come."

Since hometown therapy had been a success, this was Kel's final follow-up visit at the Mayo. Part of Kelly's treatment was massage therapy, so before leaving, Kelly asked, "Can massage spread melanoma?" Kel was told that there was no scientific proof that supported the claim, but he was never given a yes or no answer.

All I ever wanted to hear were positive reinforcements and words of hope, and I thought we were receiving them. Kel's reaction was different, and he loudly said, "They are just words." Words affected us in powerful but not always positive ways, so I reminded Kel that the oncologist was just using words when he shared his statistical bullshit. I had been called faggot more times than I ever, ever wanted to acknowledge, and I had to find my inner strength to hear it, feel it, grow from it, and find ways to accept who I was. Maybe the verbal attacks kept the closet door closed a little longer, but positive words helped build my courage, strength, and confidence to come out. No matter what words we heard, they were subject to our individual interpretation. I had confidence Kel would find positivity within the words.

When we stopped for lunch, it became obvious that Kel had listened to some words: he ate broccoli and cauliflower. Words had the ability to open our minds and create a state of heightened awareness; "I love you, Kel," was a perfect example.

## Tuesday, May 17, 2011

At 8:30 a.m., I received a call from Kel. He said, "I still have the pain but I thought, *I'll be damned if I am going to lie in bed all day when it looks so nice outside.* So I'm up." He spent the day outside, walking with Chaos and washing his car. Kel admitted that his pain had spiked to a seven (out of ten), which was unusually high for him. Instead of letting the pain debilitate him, Kelly took his time during tasks and rested when needed.

We drove Kel's spotless car to our gay friends' twenty-fifth anniversary. While others socialized, I was picturing what our celebration would look like. As I daydreamed, Kel leaned in and whispered, "I feel really good right now. The pain is gone and I can take a deep breath." His comment snapped me back into a blissful reality, and I basked in his glow and freedom from pain. Every day had inspiring moments, and we welcomed them in.

## Wednesday, May 18, 2011

If there was a guaranteed recipe for salvation, for a moment I was convinced that we would use all of the ingredients. Wouldn't everyone? Then I realized how difficult success would be. We were already aware of unhealthy foods and drinks, and yet we still succumbed to our cravings for them. Life was about living, but sometimes little indulgences could make it a lot more fun.

I would have changed Kel's entire regimen and made it as healthy as possible, but I think he would have hated his restricted life. I was looking from the outside in. I saw room for improvement rather than acknowledging the work in progress. Kel made gigantic strides in his personal acceptance, growth, and openness, but there was still part of me that wanted to see more. I wanted the best for him, and when I didn't think he was doing his best, I judged him. God, I was an asshole.

In hindsight, Kel pushed himself in efforts to get stronger and healthier. He was doing it! I didn't know what was best for him and I didn't always know what was best for me. Heck, sometimes I did know what was best and I did the opposite, just because. Neither one of us changed overnight, but we still progressed.

## Thursday, May 19, 2011

Every morning, I found myself stating, "It's going to be a good day," and then I'd say it to Kel. Turned out, it was a good day. His pride radiated when he told me he had completed his to-do list. Kel's spirits soared while the words contained a sense of self-worth. His ultimate goal was returning to work, and he was definitely rebuilding his strength and stamina in order to do so. Kelly was craving social settings, but precautions were a must while going through chemo. He referred to himself as the boy in the bubble, and if he would have been willing, I would have kept him in one. Kelly continuously reminded me to live, and that was all I wanted him to do.

## Friday, May 20, 2011

Many factors determined how we moved forward, and side effects were no exception. On Kelly's pillowcase lay the evidence that hair loss was a reality. It wasn't unexpected, but it was a shitty reminder of melanoma. Another change was being forced upon Kel but he remained present. I was proud of him.

As I left for work, Kel waved from the doorway and blew me a good-bye kiss. Happy childhood memories flooded in of my mom waving me off to school. The comforts of home had always been my safety net. When name-calling or abuse at school became intolerable, I would watch the clock and count down the time until I was safe and sound at home. As an adult, when work stressed me out, I found comfort knowing Kelly was waiting for me.

When I got home, a note reading "I heart U" waited on the door handle. Kel and I freely expressed ourselves with spoken words and supplemented with notes or kind actions. After reading his message, my mind became free of stress and I felt open to love. Stress contributed to the disconnection between my mind and body, but loving notes and actions traveled straight to my core and reunited the two. Kel's written words reminded me what was significant and important.

# Chapter Six

## Change

### Saturday, May 21, 2011

With Kelly's every step, hair was being scattered throughout the house. I told Kel it was time to cut it, and his saddened face pierced my heart when he asked, "Do I have to already?" After hours of contemplating, Kel said, "I think it's time for a head-shaving party." First, we enjoyed a great meal, accompanied by a shot of alcohol, and then Kel took control. Laughter filled our home and several photos were taken while the clippers finished what chemo started. It was a celebration of life. Kel was in the now and in control. His hair was gone and his fears were put to rest. He looked very cute with his Mr. Clean cut.

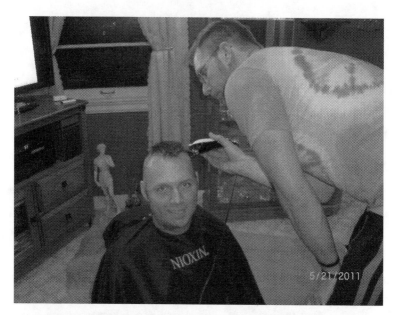

## Sunday, May 22, 2011

The saying goes, "Time flies when you're having fun." It did, and we did. The weekend laughter gave way to exhaustion. Kelly slept much of the day, and at 8:00 p.m., I told him to get his ass up so we could go for walk. A short jaunt later, I realized I just wanted to relax with both Kel and Chaos. Caring Bridge updates were brushed aside, and our traditional Sunday— movie day—resumed. Being near Kelly had a way of making me feel stronger than ever. I was aware and conscious, believing we could achieve whatever we sought.

## Monday, May 23, 2011

Kelly's new look received numerous positive responses, and I felt it increased his confidence. He looked healthier, his eyes were bright, and his smile was genuine.

During work, I was continually asked about Kelly's health, but this was the first day I was tearlessly able to speak with positive truths. Kel and I had experienced mental moments free of cancer but it was rare for me to talk, free of tears, about melanoma. Sharing Kel's story and my perspective was a fortunate outlet that assisted my personal growth. He may have had some pain-filled days, but his ability to overcome was an inspiring testament I liked to share.

## Tuesday, May 24, 2011

Kelly woke in pain, but he dragged his butt out of bed and moved to the couch. As time passed, so did the clouds, and a blue sky emerged and awakened his spirits. Kel took Chaos for a walk and absorbed some of the sun's love. He appreciated something we had overlooked for years: the sun's power to energize us.

The very things that made Kel and I feel good were potential causes of anguish. Pick your poison: tanning beds or the sun. We basked in the sun, soaking up every ray we could attract, and old pictures depict our unawareness. We were so tan and we unintentionally looked older. I used to think I looked good: my teeth seemed whiter and my eye color popped. I also acknowledged the tightness of my face and how much more pronounced the lines around my eyes were. Hearing, "You look so tan," or, "You are so dark," was music to my ears because I assumed they were compliments. I shouldn't have assumed, and I was an ass in doing so. I remember my response when people would voice their suntan warnings: "Eventually I'm going to get old and ugly, so I may as well look as good as I can right now!" At the time, much of that statement felt honest, but Kelly's diagnosis changed our tanning days forever. We were no longer abusing, but we were definitely enjoying every sunny day.

**Kelly depicts his broadmindedness and determination in each of these e-mails.**

*Before my cancer, I was never much of a religious person, but it has opened my mind to praying. I guess what I'm getting at is, I'm praying.*

\*\*\*

*Fruits and vegetables are still a struggle, but we plan to try kale tonight. We were given a recipe where you cook it in the oven and it crisps like a potato chip (who would have ever guessed). On the lighter side, my new haircut has been a hit with many, so that has made the transition much easier. I think it has actually made Joe hornier, because he has been grabbing me like crazy ever since. Ha!*

\*\*\*

*Thanks for taking the time to write me. I always appreciate and hold on to stories from those who have actually had cancer. I can't tell you how many times I have been approached with stories where the person tells me what is best for me because a "friend of a friend" (that one always kills me) had something similar. I completely agree that attitude is everything, and seeing family cry gives me strength to fight. On another note, when weakness tries to take over, I have stated numerous times, "Kelly, you are not a selfish person! You will feel better and you must live for the simple fact of not hurting others." I know you really don't know me, but I'm a very upbeat and positive person who won't accept anything but life as my outcome. I'm gonna beat this even if it kills me.* Not! *Ha! A little humor that Joe doesn't seem to appreciate. Thanks for being an inspiration!*

## Wednesday, May 25, 2011

Kelly: "I don't know how you are doing this Joe. You're working so hard. I couldn't do it." Me: "Are you kidding me? What I am doing is a piece of cake. Working is like a prize compared to what you are going through. I don't know how you are doing it!"

From bed, Kel looked at me and said, "Today will be a good day. It isn't starting off that way, but it will be!" As he uttered the words, I could sense the pain he was dealing with: spikes of eight or nine out of ten. Pain definitely lacked respect or sympathy. Kel almost cancelled his arm therapy appointment, but he hoped getting out of the house would bring him some relief. It did, but the cancer still brought bouts of fatigue, sweats, and chills. During every phone conversation, Kel acknowledged his pain and maintained his positive attitude.

Some days were mentally and physically draining, but all of the ugliness was powerless against our hope.

## Thursday, May 26, 2011

Kelly's sleep suffered and eating was sporadic, but he continued to crack (what he thought were) funny jokes. A deep breath, a jolt, or a bump on the road caused him to flinch and moan. A short jaunt from the car to the Mayo Clinic elevators made him short of breath and affected his speech. Kelly's pain was too intense, and chemo treatment number four was postponed. A CAT scan was needed in order to calm fears and gain facts.

Before the CAT scan, we checked ourselves into a hotel that was attached to the Mayo Clinic. The pain was too severe for Kel to walk, so I ended up pushing him by wheelchair. At first, we were both taken aback by his need for a chair, but Kelly's comfort was our only concern. As he rode to each appointment, his vulnerabilities were worn on his sleeve, and I was so proud of him.

In order to keep his weight on, Kelly was told to eat whatever he wanted. With food in our bellies, we headed back to our room. Pain still had its grasp on Kelly, but he was able to slowly walk to our destinations. A phone call confirmed the scan was clear of blood clots; therefore, Kelly was a victim of pain without a cause. We rested on the bed in hopes of taking a nap, but the pain spiked and Kel looked like he was going crazy. After demanding more meds, I held his hands and we talked. Slowly, his frenzy subsided. I was searching internally for an explanation for this madness, when my eyes became fixated on the T-shirts we wore. The words on mine read, "This is my lucky shirt." I was very lucky, because Kelly was my partner. Kel wore his Tonka shirt; he was tough like a Tonka truck. Together, we were lucky and tough, and there was an incredible power source between us!

## Friday, May 27, 2011

Throughout the night and this morning, Kelly's sentences were hard to decipher. Two words, one word, a sound—nothing was making sense. When I questioned him, he got frustrated and said he was just mumbling. After three nights of sleeplessness, Kel was becoming someone I didn't recognize. I just wanted him to share everything so we could talk about the issues and use the knowledge to fight. Before bed, he said, "I feel like I would go to bed and not wake up. It would be wrong, not saying good-bye." We laid down at 10:30 p.m. Kel's eyes were rolling up in his head as his lids were closing. At 1:30 a.m., Kel's jerking and twitching woke me. I was also lacking sleep and my frustration reared its ugly head, which only added to Kelly's stress. I tried to talk him off the ledge and regain control: 2:30 a.m. ... 2:55 a.m. ... 3:23 a.m. ... I had a new suggestion at every waking moment, and I put forth all my efforts to help him find sleep. All night, Kelly would go ten seconds without taking a breath and then he would take a small gasp of air. When he would wake, he would feel as if he had slept all night, but in reality, the REM state was never achieved. What else could I do except listen, watch, hope, and pray? I bawled. The alarm went off at 6:40 a.m. and both of us felt as if the last hours of sleep were solid.

Due to the natural progression of Kel's melanoma, we were told that chemo was necessary. Pain still persisted as I wheeled him to treatment, and I was unaware of any other way I could assist him. Liquid Benadryl was finally taking over, and Kel was finding some peace and sleep. Because he also had a fever, fluids were administered through IV to assist with dehydration. Before long, Kel was sawing logs and was soaked head to toe with sweat. The nurse changed the chemo line in his hand and was surprised that he slept through it. Every nurse who walked by his room commented on his snoring, and I breathed a sigh of relief that he had reached REM. But suddenly and with a look of urgency on his face, he sat up and said, "I need to pee." We barely got him to the bathroom. I went back to his room, and it was impossible to miss his sweaty body print on the sheets. It was also apparent that Kelly's hair follicles were unable to support the weight of even the shortest of hairs; his white pillow case was speckled with fallout. If Kelly scratched his head, hair sprinkled down around him. The nurse rejoined us, and I told her Kel's coloring became ten times better after his fever broke. She looked at me and said, "So did yours." We all laughed because it was the truth. Chemo was completed. Kel and I walked out together.

A quick rest was needed during our walk back to the hotel, but it sure felt awesome to gain so much ground. I had every reason to believe our drive home would be better than the ride to the Mayo Clinic. It was, because Kel slept most of the way home. I think I chuckled aloud once or twice as I embraced the simple pleasures of life that surrounded me.

Thirty-seven hours can feel like a week, and yet that is precisely how long our trip was—the most action-packed, physically charged, and emotionally draining thirty-seven-hour trip we had ever taken. Home felt very good. Higher medication doses kept pain under control, but Kelly's balance was challenged until he adjusted to the new dosage. His sweats became a sign of hope; as soon as the fever broke, he felt better. We were back, humor was soaring, spirits were on the rise, his attitude was proactive, and communication was solid.

In bed by 10:30 p.m., we situated the pillows so the air could flow in and out with hopes of keeping Kelly comfortable. We must have had things aligned perfectly because he slept. I wasn't sure what time I nodded off, but I remembered waking to the delightful sound of his snoring. I disliked snoring, but this time it succeeded multiple sleepless nights and actually assisted my sleep.

These thirty-seven hours were a turning point for me. I became aware that my inability to stop Kel's pain and suffering had little bearing on the impact I could make. I was his partner, cheerleader, supporter, etc., and we would move forward, as always, utilizing our newfound knowledge and awareness. We had the power to change, direct, and create what we wanted our future to look like, and that included dancing, singing, and loving life!

## Saturday, May 28, 2011

During the morning, we chatted about the previous days, recapping the highs and lows, the good and the bad, things we did right and what needed improvement, and everything in between. That afternoon, Kel was back in bed, and it wasn't long before I heard his snores. Our evening was a vacation from our concerns as we laughed away hours as if they were minutes.

At bedtime, Kel was propped up with pillows, and I think it helped with his overall quality of sleep. He hardly snored, and his breathing had a peaceful flow. Sleep followed an in-depth conversation, and I felt we became even closer. Before closing our eyes, we spoke our hopes and desires: "Tomorrow is going to be a great day." Forward thinking and happy thoughts paved our road into dreamland.

# Sunday, May 29, 2011

We both slept great, and upon waking, we continued the previous night's conversation. *Scared* and *afraid* were the words Kel used to describe himself. It became apparent pain had really taken its toll on his psyche, and doubt was a natural companion. I wanted Kelly to openly share his fears so their hold would lessen. He had a realization this could potentially be his last Memorial Day weekend, and fear entered his consciousness. I questioned if anyone could be unscathed by that thought. Emotions were affected or triggered by just about everything, and working through them proved to be a changing equation.

Kelly felt crying was a weakness, but for me, tears were easy to shed and always brought uncertain amounts of clarity. Sometimes they could be painful to expel, but they washed away my sadness or sorrow; at other times, they were the result of my pure happiness. No matter their cause or purpose, tears cleansed the body, mind, and soul. They are a portal for emotions, and I believed they flushed out toxins that could further poison a body. If I could have proven tears heal, tear-dammed individuals would view crying as an intelligent release rather than a weakness. There wasn't any reason to question a teardrop's purpose or a need to stop a natural human form of expression.

One year from this date, we planned to repeat our adventures of today, reflecting and acknowledging the power of a visualized future. The day we would relive included a car ride, visiting loved ones, walking with Chaos, and enjoying each moment together. Every one of these experiences was discussed the night before. We made them happen, and it was a great day! In one year, those experiences would be a celebration.

It was impossible to know or understand everything about Kelly because, throughout his life, he was continually learning about himself. Kel and I shared pieces of our painful history and acknowledged what they taught us. Every blow to our esteem and every ounce of love we received had shaped and molded who we became. We were proud of ourselves and one another. We knew our reality and we were exactly where we were supposed to be. But from now on, we planned to visualize where we wanted to go.

## Monday, May 30, 2011

Late morning, Kel was in a deep sleep, the deepest I had ever witnessed—even deeper than a drunken sleep. I sat next to him and spoke wishes and wants. My hope was that they'd enter his subconscious and take captive the pollutants in his body. My understanding of subliminal messaging was nonexistent, but I proceeded as if I were a pro. I planned on speaking to every level of consciousness until I was heard. Sometimes as I spoke, Kel would exert a loud snore as if he were trying to interrupt me. Other times, his eyes would dart behind his lids and his tongue would move inside his mouth as if he wanted to respond to my words. I knew I was being heard.

As the three-day weekend came to a close, our appreciation for life radiated. Memorial Day had impacted us differently this year. My sympathy, appreciation, and lack of understanding consumed my core while Kelly faced mortality. We visited burial sites of relatives, friends, and acquaintances, and while we stood at the Veteran's Memorial, I found myself questioning war. It seemed ironic that we had a personal war going on, but questioning why would have been irrelevant. My emotions fluctuated throughout the day, and I shielded my tears from Kelly. It was a day to honor, and yet I was unable to fully comprehend why lives had to be taken this way. Kelly was at war, and we knew there were personal battles ahead. With understanding and preparation, we thought we would be victorious. We believed in what we were fighting for. I began to understand the meaning behind Memorial Day: people fought for something they believed in, and not everyone survived.

We shared moments when laughter overpowered pain, and, while sitting near each other, felt blanketed with peace. Future thoughts only contained happy outcomes.

"Anything is possible, if you try!" - inspiring words from the Electric Sunshine Man.

## Tuesday, May 31, 2011

One moment can speak volumes; this one did.

Kel and I had just taken Chaos for a walk, and as we walked to the car, he said, "I feel good, Joe. I feel very good!" Nothing else about the day was worth mentioning because this moment transcended all.

## Wednesday, June 1, 2011

Before heading off to work, I said my usual, "It's going to be a good day," and Kel looked at me and said, "It's going to be a fabulous day!" His pain was minimal, and his spirits were flying with the kites. Later that morning, I called Kelly, and he said "I feel like I'm sitting around waiting to see if it's going to be a good day or a bad day." Good or bad was purely based upon his pain level. Fatigue could slow him down, but pain was potentially debilitating. Kel realized he was waiting to be controlled rather than taking control. Was this a revelation or a higher state of awareness? Either way, he was prepared to fly high again.

Inspiring resources found their way into our home, and we chose to incorporate some of their teachings. Just like a snowflake, we were special and unique; our structure varied as much as our beliefs. I added teachings if they supplemented my personal growth, and Kel adopted practices that fit within his realm of belief. Whatever we chose, we chose it with intent to enhance our lives. Our faith expanded with our resources. Knowledge was power, and we were plugged in.

## Friday, June 3, 2011

Early in the day, Kel was very sleepy, but he gained momentum and ended on a high note. Pain was still present, but it was closer to gone. Post-surgery sites were becoming less distinct, and wrist flexibility had greatly increased. Emotional healing was challenging to gauge, but every time he yelled, I knew he was improving. Head acne was the most obvious chemo side-effect, and like a rash, it became very painful.

After twelve and a half hours of travel (including chemo), we were welcomed home by a power outage. Lanterns and candles lit our quarters, but our house-cleaning intentions were put on hold. Power was restored after two hours, and we spent the next hours bringing our home to light, so to speak. Our house hadn't been cleaned like this in months, and Kel's stamina was impressive. Kelly was affected but stronger, altered but enhanced.

**Kelly and I drew up an agreement, and then he e-mailed me our pact:**

*What I (Kelly) can do for Joe:*
*1) Try my best to get the nutrients, calories, exercise, and rest.*
*2) Understand that my personal decisions affect Joe.*
*3) Work on communication!*

*What Joe can do for Kelly:*
*1) Read aloud each new CB entry and discuss prior to hitting Post.*
*2) Understand that personal decisions affect Kelly.*
*3) Work on communication!*

*I love you!*

## Saturday, June 4, 2011

Just after 1:00 a.m., we went to bed. The alarm was set for 8:30 a.m., allowing enough time for any finishing touches before company arrived. Once Kelly woke, every sentence he spoke poured forth with positivity. He got out of bed and said, "Look at me," and he proceeded to do numerous jumping jacks. Pain had previously made it impossible for Kel to do any form of jumping, but all day he was pain-free. I wondered if the removal of dust and dirt from our home cleared some of Kel's pain triggers. Our home was revitalized, and Kel was rejuvenated. Was it possible that cleaning reenergized positive forces within the household and us?

We celebrated the beauty of life, love, and nature, stepping into the world and out of our lives of consumption. It was a day filled with experiences that exhausted us by 1:00 a.m.

## Sunday, June 5, 2011

What prompted such an incredible weekend? We were looking forward to it; one week prior, we decided that it was going to be a great weekend. The puzzle pieces of life came together in unison, creating the big picture.

## Monday, June 6, 2011

I read there is a 75 percent increased risk of getting melanoma for tanning-bed users. Before January, I'm unsure if I could have defined melanoma, but I was certainly blind to the statistics. Unfortunately, Kel had to become a statistic before we changed our tanning habits. While sitting on our deck, I freaked when I noticed my farmer's tan was actually red. I was never a sunscreen advocate, but I was becoming one. When the sun shined, we were brighter too, but now we were protecting ourselves. Old habits were replaced with consciousness.

Kel's ability to remain active for longer periods of time was impressive. His attitude and vitality allowed me to forget any ailment was part of his life. I asked myself, "Is his ailment gone?" I mentally answered, *Soon*. I looked back just long enough to acknowledge how far we had traveled, and then forward we went.

**In this e-mail, Kelly was answering questions about his return to work and Minneapolis Gay Pride weekend plans:**

*I haven't returned to work yet because of the clearing process of all my meds. I actually have enjoyed the extra couple of days off because I know there will be lots for me to catch up on! And I know that nicer weather is right around the corner. Ha! The "no check" thing for the past five weeks, however, has been ish, and thank God for the benefit and everyone's help (thanks)! Earlier today, I mentioned to Joe that the Monday after Pride might not be possible this year. I will have zero vacation time and will feel awkward asking for a day when I've just returned. There are thoughts that we will stay Friday and Saturday versus Saturday and Sunday. Who knows, work might drive me crazy and I might just say, "F it," and ask for that Monday off anyway. If there is a descent music act, that might help me get the courage also, but right now my focus needs to be on getting back. Hope to talk with ya soon!*

## Wednesday, June 8, 2011

Even on pain-free, active days, there were trials and tribulations that needed attending to. It felt as if minute concerns were using time and energy that could have—should have—been used to fight for his life. However, once these concerns were put to rest, we were able and prepared to focus on the main attraction: life. It was absolutely our objective. Kelly's health may have become the deciding factor for every future plan, and I may have had to process our limitations in my own way, but we were in it together. We didn't always operate like a perfectly fine-tuned machine, but that was when our relationship exhibited the most growth. Our big picture, our ultimate goal, our main focus always remained the same: Kelly's remission.

Kel and I went into our hot tub to relax, but instead, my mind raced with questions. *How has he been able to handle having his entire life and identity altered? Would I be able to go about life the same as he?* As my thoughts traveled from past moments to present situations, I analyzed the way I had been handling our current situation. It was then I realized how much writing had become my outlet. Caring Bridge had become a way for me to free my pain during an awful situation that could have swallowed me whole. Sharing became a way to trample the negative thoughts with words of hope and clarity. Melanoma had forever altered the way Kel and I would live our lives, and we weren't going to live kicking and screaming, "Why, oh why?" We were two individuals who found an opportunity within every moment!

## Thursday, June 9, 2011

Exhausting Moment: Our drive (to and from the Mayo Clinic) and appointments were fourteen hours of focus and purpose.

Teary Moment: During chemo, our room was shared with another fellow and his companion. The fellow's age was undetectable because his appearance was weathered from cancer. His energy level was very low, and his voice was quiet and withdrawn. He was polite and willing to do what he could. After his treatment, he was feeble and had to be placed in his wheelchair. He was a complete stranger, and yet within the first thirty seconds, Kel and I had opinions, reactions, questions, etc. He was a solemn sight to digest, and we felt sympathetic and emotional, inside and out.

Possible Moment: That fellow may have been living out the best part of his life. Maybe he was a bundle of emotional energy and joy when he was in his safe environment.

Bottom Line Moment: A story was created based upon what we saw, assumed, judged, and predicted. Positive thoughts have the ability to overpower negativity, but it is seldom the choice made.

Funny Moment: I looked at Kel and said, "Right now, that fellow is talking to his companion, saying 'Did you see that pathetic-looking dude who came into our room? He's a mess! And how about that sad-looking thing that was getting the chemo? I'm damn lucky I'm not either one of them!'"

Realistic Moment: Another couple entered our room, and the guy immediately began to share his story. Chemo was going very well, but the benefits plateaued. He had two weeks to consider his options and admitted he was discouraged. After acknowledging he needed to stop being negative, his gal pal sounded off with "Uh-huh." As he pleaded his case for consistency, I told him the one constant that he could have at every moment was his attitude. Gal pal sounded off with "Uh-huh." Kel was more than ready to remove himself from the room and the underwhelming positivity.

Unexpected Moment: A dermatology appointment was added to Kel's schedule. Because Kelly was experiencing pain and itching from his acne rash, they wanted to examine and treat him. Profuse sweating and a chemo drug were probable causes for his flare-ups. Kel left with another prescription.

Delusional Moment: After his dose of liquid Benadryl, Kel was very tired. His eyes were wide open, and he said, "Good thing they have puppy boxes here."

I said, "Huh? What?" He repeated himself, and we both started laughing. Kelly told me that he was sleeping with his eyes open when he made the comment. Later, he informed me puppy boxes were areas where you can pet animals. I was still adapting to Kel's random thoughts and incomplete sentences. They confused me and made my mind work double-time. They also made us laugh.

Informational Moment: Kelly had options. New melanoma-fighting drugs were available, and Kel had to decide whether to choose a different course of action or stay in the clinical study. The study coordinator explained that the drug he was currently taking was similar to the newly available drugs. She also said, "This is going to work for you," and Kelly stayed in the study. We walked the stepping stones of life; each step added to our foundation.

My Moment: Picturing the worst allowed the worst to manifest and take shape. Imagining the best left no room for a negative outcome.

## Friday, June 10, 2011

An example of determination and perseverance, Kelly returned to work. He worked six hours, and I only received one text: "I'm doing/feeling really good!" It was all I needed to go about my day with confidence and ease, motivated by Kel's personal drive.

# Sunday, June 12, 2011

It was beautiful weekend weather. Surrounded by love, time moved swiftly while memories were created. Thoughts of writing were close to my heart, but living in the moment took precedence. Mother Nature had been kind on our weekends, and we clocked several hours outside on our deck. I absorbed some vitamin D while Kel, protected from the sun, napped in a chair across from me. We were breathing in fresh air, which filled our world with life.

With life, there were *good* and *could be better* moments. My patience had been stretched farther than ever before, and it was difficult for me to overcome. I would have rated myself five out of ten for effectively remaining patient with Kel. Even though his personal growth was unparalleled to any other I had witnessed, my expectations had become concentrated and prevalent. I wanted Kel to do every positive, possible thing at every moment; like a chameleon, he adapted to each challenge. Kel seemed to weigh the cause and effect before arriving at a decision.

My mother told me I have a "got to have it now" personality. If I feel it, wish it, dream it, want it, I will do whatever it takes to get it. She was right, and what I wanted was Kel's perfect health. My "got to have it now" charm had previously been used on material items, but Kelly's value was priceless. I wondered, "Could the phrase 'I feel like a million bucks' be representative of the purchase price for Kel's health?" If words can wound, wouldn't they also have the ability to heal? Every positive resource was similar to currency. We tried to buy Kel's perfect health with love, knowledge and change.

# Chapter Seven

## The Working Man

### Monday, June 13, 2011

Because Kel was sleeping six to eight hours each night, his nightly pain meds were being missed. Obviously, his med schedule changed day by day and was determined by his waking hour. Skipping doses was not advised, but it demonstrated Kelly's pain progress. When he'd wake, minor throat irritation and facial pain were his biggest annoyances. We were cautiously optimistic we would not fall behind on pain control, and sound sleep felt like it was worth the risk.

Once again, Chaos had two working daddies. I was positive he'd miss the daily companionship, but I knew he would adapt. Kelly worked six hours, and it was apparent he was tired. I was concerned he would overwork himself, but I had to trust he'd respect his capabilities. I used vacation days during every obstacle we faced, and coworkers were anxious for my full-time status. My physical return was full-force but my mind was at 75 percent, while Kel's return was part-time with a 100 percent mind requirement. We both took pride in our work, but Kelly's health was top priority.

## Tuesday, June 14, 2011

Kel and I were up until early morning hours trying to alleviate Chaos's ear annoyance, but our efforts only supplied sympathy. While his eyes begged for a solution, Chaos was seeking comfort and refuge from us. We did the best we could with the knowledge we had, and eventually we fell asleep. I took Chaos to the vet and received the answer that eluded us: he had an earwax plug.

Earwax or melanoma, the need to cure my loved one's ailments felt very much the same. With yanked heart strings, my life's balance remained off-kilter until I gained perspective. During their times of woe, my lack of control felt normal, but control was never mine to begin with. The only thing I could control was how the future looked in my mind: harmonious balance for our family of three.

## Wednesday, June 15, 2011

I awoke to the sound of smacking lips and what might have been grinding teeth. It actually sounded gross, so I woke Kel and asked, "Were you grinding your teeth?" He wasn't. "What was the sound you were making?" I inquired.

He responded, "I was eating cookies!" I laughed, and within thirty seconds, he was back to sleep. Later in the morning Kel called me just to say, "I feel tiptop."

Gone were Kel's days of sitting around the house, attempting to forecast his pain. He had four days of work under his belt, and each was followed by hours of sleep. This time, after he woke, we watched *The Real Housewives*. I felt it should air as a self-help show on PBS, because it reminded me what not to do or say, how not to act, and why I was proud of Kel and me. Throughout 2011, we educated ourselves and learned to focus on the positives and possibilities. TRH was a testament to our individual and partnered growth that we could feel, see, and hear.

Caring Bridge was the place to update and inform, and with that came weighted emotions. Thankfully, we had become light in the loafers, and emotional baggage was temporarily unpacked. Sharing lighthearted narratives was one way to tip the scales and offer a happier tale. Unlike the housewives, our lives were not always based upon drama, and it felt important to share that. We were proud to be light in the loafers, which was never a bad thing.

## Saturday, June 18, 2011

With almost thirty hours worked, Kel completed his first full week. Each day, he was reacquainted with the familiar routine. I was proud of his courage, strength, confidence, and attitude. But I also witnessed exhaustion and fatigue.

Kel and I had an evening of emotional frustration, which lacked any reason. This could have led us down a spiraled, miserable path, but we found our footing and stepped into consciousness. We stopped the negative energy flow and welcomed in positivity. We had a choice; it was ours to own, and all we had to do was decide upon it. Positive or negative, whatever we declared became a welcome mat for more of the same.

When life was in balance, it felt like stabilizers continued to enter our world. I started recognizing that when things were great, more great things happened. Sadly, negativity also had the same results.

## Monday, June 20, 2011

I was clueless what Stage IV melanoma looked like, because I only ever saw the man I loved. When I looked at Kelly, I was unaware that he had an expiration date because he overflowed with life. Kel's existence, in its entirety, was altered beyond my comprehension, and I found myself appraising life's pleasures. By this time of year, Kel and I had typically enjoyed two sunny vacations. Our carefree time together was the thing I was missing most because every aspect of our current life required us to be responsible. While my mind revisited former traveling days, I realized much of my past existence was time wished away rather than appreciating every moment. I used to mentally fast-forward through life, daydreaming about future plans and wishing I was somewhere else. Kelly's diagnosis kept me present, and the future gave us hope.

Present and alert, Kel was really wearing on my nerves, and I am sure he was getting tired of me. Weekend separations were common in our relationship, so we went our separate ways and spent time with our families. Our time apart was used to regroup while surrounding ourselves with familiar, safe settings. I was happy and proud to be by Kelly's side, but sometimes we had to take time and breathe our own air.

## Tuesday, June 21, 2011

*Beware, what lies ahead are no puns, no humor, and no in-depth stories. Joe has taken the night off, so you're stuck with me (Kelly). Ha!*

*OMG! If you were to tell me a year back that someday I would enjoy a zucchini, apple, celery, and carrot juice drink via juicer, I would have told you ,"You're crazy!" Boy, how time can change a person, and so I want those who think they are stuck in a rut to know that change* can happen!

*As for now, me and Joe are ready for whatever is thrown our way regarding the scan results. I have felt really good the past few weeks (as long as I stay ahead of my meds), and positivity has played a huge role in all of it.*

*As we hear things, Joe will keep you updated!*

*Love to all and thanks for being with me during all of this!*

*Kelly*

## Wednesday, June 22, 2011

After reading Kel's Caring Bridge post, I had to chuckle. I had begun juicing one week prior, and I had made up my mind that Kel was going to drink my concoctions. The very first time I juiced, I started drinking it in hopes of manipulating his opposition. When I handed him the glass, he took a sip after giving me a sour look of disgust. He wasn't impressed, but he drank half because he believed it could help. The following morning, he was woken by me, holding a glass of juice. Boy, was he annoyed, and he shouted, "I am not going to drink this every morning!" But this time, he drank more than half. Day three, I added more ice so it was much colder, and he drank all but two sips. Day four, he said, "Mmm this is good!" A few days before he posted on CB, he asked if I was going to make juice. Like I said, I made up my mind that Kel was going to drink it, but I never expected him to ask for it.

When Kelly returned to work, he tried to convince me that my Caring Bridge updates were no longer needed. Several coworkers had been following his CB status, and current posts were complicating the professionalism he wanted to restore. We made an agreement: I would only post on CB after his stamp of approval, and he promised to have a fiber bar and an Ensure every morning. I was much better with the follow-through.

On the surface, we were calm, cool, and collected. Awareness of the subconscious was drowned out by thought while positive mental pictures replayed in my noggin, defusing any negativity. Everything is right when there is no other choice. We were back in Rochester, and checked in; blood was drawn and new scans were taken. Kel and I were already moving past the day because we had a party to attend. Life!

## Thursday, June 23, 2011

When I heard the news, tears crept from my eyes. First, the doctor asked Kelly how he was feeling, and then he said, "To be honest, looking at you and hearing what you're saying tells me more than the scans do." Every lung tumor had shrunk, and one previous spot was now undetectable. Unfortunately, the tumor that caused the most pain shrunk the least. Only one tumor on his liver shrank while every other expanded in size. A radiologist explained that fluid increased around the cancer that was being destroyed; therefore each tumor became enlarged. It appeared as if the clinical study was working; after all, every scan result was accompanied by a positive explanation.

Kelly asked, "Would you say that I am average, below average, or better than average?"

With zero hesitation, his doctor replied, "Better than average."

During the ride home and before Kel fell asleep, we expressed our emotions. Kelly admitted he wanted to be better than above average and he wanted to hear the doctor say, "Wow, Kelly, you are blowing us away with the tumor shrinkage and the fact some are gone." This became our wish, our goal, and our will, so we discussed ways to refine our choices and decisions for a greater impact. We continued collecting information and expanding our knowledge, which increased our strengths and beliefs. Perfection may have been impossible, but there were ways to bring us closer to it.

## Saturday, June 25, 2011

Everyone could chart his/her course of life the exact same way, like mindless individuals, but Kel and I ventured out and discovered riches. Our most action-packed, plan-oriented weekend since 2010 was upon us. Minneapolis Gay Pride was among one of our outings, and like many events, it took on a new meaning and feeling. For Kelly, he was making a fresh appearance as he moved forth with great confidence. I was grateful that we had this weekend to openly celebrate many aspects of pride. We were out, and with our family and friends surrounding us, we radiated gay pride and gratitude.

We were both a little anxious and nervous for our first nightclub outing. I was on high-alert, ready to protect and defend Kelly, while he was more passive than usual. Within minutes, we found our niche, and as protective walls crumbled, our personalities emerged. With friends around, a comfortable setting was created and conversations flowed naturally. Several people loved Kelly's new crew-cut, and some asked why he chose the hairstyle. Kel simply explained a medical condition made the decision for him. We also ran into friends who hadn't previously heard about Kel's cancer, and their support was immediately extended. There were questions and tears, but Kel and I met them with optimism.

I wanted everyone to look at Kel, taking a really long look at him. Forever changed externally and internally, Kelly was a better man because of his acceptance and openness. During this cancer crisis, I altered my thought process and subconsciously became a happier person. I focused on positive thoughts and found my overall perspective had flourished. Resources made themselves present but change was our conscious effort and decision.

## Monday, June 27, 2011

One month prior, I had read about visualization: the act of visualizing what you want. I immediately started picturing Kel and me dancing at Gay Pride. Because of Kelly's health, we considered skipping the entire weekend, but I continued to visualize our dance. One week before the weekend events, Kel called me and said, "Joe, we need a vacation; we deserve some fun. Let's go to Pride." Sunday evening, Exposé performed, and Kel and I were dancing. Needless to say, I was beaming that my visualization became reality.

Kel and I were fully aware that Gay Pride was going to be different this year. It was our first Pride when time was a luxury rather than a tightly packed schedule. The need to stop, drop, and sleep was a question of *when* rather than *if*. Every decision should have been Kel's, but he sacrificed his well-being in order for me to have a carefree weekend. It was different from any other Pride, but I was never more proud of Kel.

## Wednesday, June 29, 2011

Kelly was juggling work, household responsibilities, quality family time, and moments for him, while taking care of any health woes that happened to intrude. I had to continually remind myself that Kel was facing major obstacles and differences. He tried to adhere to a schedule, but what kept him balanced changed day by day. Almost every single activity was visualized with hopes of being physically able to successfully accomplish it. Naturally, there were unforeseen challenges, but whatever attempted to knock Kel down was never able to dismantle his balance.

We were adjusting to an ever-changing schedule and reestablishing our partnered roles. I may have been a bitch at times, but I would have done anything to restore Kel's health. Kelly did as much as he could but was disappointed he couldn't do more. If there was a prescription for a perfectly balanced day, I desperately wanted it. Our relationship felt like we were walking on tightropes more than basking in balance. We were products of our environment, and it felt like intruders were beginning to separate us. I wondered if our synchronicity would return if we isolated ourselves from the world. Was there any way of escaping outside turmoil while maintaining a harmonious relationship? When we shared one of our daily rituals (walking), we reconnected and balance returned. We were fortunate to have discovered a way of neutralizing our obsessive, behavioral actions.

Balance was only attained when we reacted positively to negativity. Contentment within our capabilities brought satisfaction without expectation. Listening, not just with our ears, assisted our decisions and encouraged us to move forth. Eating food that fueled our bodies impacted how we existed, while exercising both body and mind kept us sharp and quick. We had the prescription; we just needed reminding.

## Thursday, June 30, 2011

We went shopping before chemo, and Kel said, "I want to get things so that I can enjoy them while I am here. Who knows how long I have?" I supported his desire to buy things for enjoyment, but I didn't want him doubting his longevity. Strangely, questioning his life expectancy released his guilt that accompanied his spending habits. If he lost his battle, Kel wanted to make sure I was financially stable. Therefore, happily spending money was a major struggle for him. I encouraged him to spend freely and asked him, "Can I buy you back if I lose you?" My only concern was his health. Sadly, Kelly's money and financial concerns were his main reason for returning to work.

"The glamorous life of chemotherapy!" was a quote from Kelly as he sat for a photo op. During Kel's journey, pictures became just as important as the written word. While he received chemo, Kelly asked me to take a photo so he could share it with his mom and dad. There were many other places we would have rather been, but Kel's smile lit up just the same. Chemo treatment was our reality, and we gratefully appreciated the potentially life-extending effects.

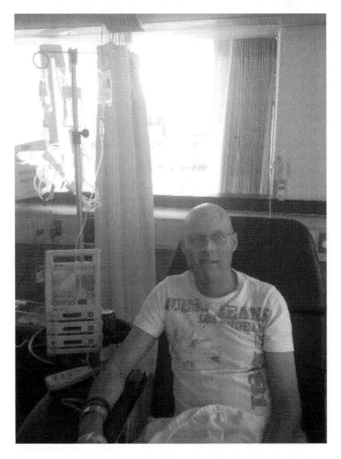

On our travels home, our senses were engaged by things that were out of our control. The sky was blue, the air was warm, fields of green surrounded us, and bright, colorful flowers shared their beauty and aromas. I took a deep breath and sighed. I felt balanced.

## Tuesday, July 5, 2011.

Our days had been spent with family and friends, and the opinions of all seemed unanimous: Kel looked great. His strength and stamina had increased, and it felt like he was on his way to a full recovery. There were moments I forgot about the havoc melanoma had wreaked. Combining my rigid, stern regimen and Kel's loose yet conscious process appeared to be successful.

Kel and I had regularly watched a television series based on a woman's fight against cancer. We knew the series was based on real events, and during this particular episode, the main character announced she had Stage IV melanoma. The words stabbed my heart, and tears welled in my eyes. Kelly's emotions mirrored mine, and the TV show represented our life. The premise for the series emulated our journey. They both focused on living.

Before updating Caring Bridge with a new writing (which was similar to the previous paragraphs), I shared my words with Kel. He cried out, "It's too much!" I was confused and baffled by his reaction. Was Kelly embarrassed by his emotions? Did he have a different outlook I was unwilling to acknowledge? Had he started to give up or was this his way of taking control? He may have felt I was sharing too much, but I felt like neither of us was doing enough. I questioned his decisions, judged his intentions, and expected more. My lack of control made me desperate to try and gain it. It was impossible to support Kelly while I was constantly trying to alter his methods. My support was the only thing Kel wanted, and in my blindness, I believed he was throwing it away. This was the first time I wanted to quit.

## Wednesday, July 6, 2011

Kel believed everyone should keep their private life private and their personal life personal. When I began writing in Caring Bridge, my intent was to inform and unite the readers so a collective positive energy would surround us. In my writings, I shared much of our lives because I was an open book and I truly believed what I shared would and could only be used for good. Many of Kelly's coworkers were following his progress and began to know him on a very intimate level. This was difficult for Kel, and I was in denial that my writings were having a negative effect on him at work. We had several CB discussions, and he was adamant I decrease the amount I shared. He informed me that one individual approached him and said, "Joe is exploiting you on Caring Bridge." Words had a way of directly impacting Kelly's fears, and this was no exception. That comment really affected him, and I was devastated anyone could have taken my writings and twisted them in such an ugly way. Shortly after that comment, I ceased my writings and passed creative control of CB onto Kel.

It had only been one week since my updates had stopped, but I felt the bond between readers becoming unglued. Missing were updates encouraging and guiding those who loved and cared about us. The energy previously put forth felt as if it was displaced in the universe. Sharing and writing helped me grow and gain perspective, and I believed it was doing the same for our supporters. As much as I didn't understand Kel's CB stance, his health remained my main objective and I wanted to reduce his stress, not be the source of it.

# Chapter Eight

# The Unread Pages: Raw and Emotional

## Wednesday, July 6, 2011

When Kel learned CB was under his reign, he said, "This will be better for you!" I wondered if he faithfully read what I had written, because I certainly didn't see how this was better for either of us. I was frustrated and saddened that something I believed was very positive had ended. In his social settings, Kelly sought fun, and his aversion to drama was his right. Though I was writing honestly, the words were reiterating the drama Kel was trying to step away from. There was no escape when his story was known by almost everyone he faced.

Kel had been exhibiting nontypical, unattractive behaviors, and during our family walk, he began insulting the appearance of others. I think he expected me to laugh, but instead I thought, *Look in a mirror. I'm guessing your feelings would be hurt if they made rude comments about you.* I remembered a theory stating, "When you ridicule another, it is an attempt to feel better about your own inadequacies."

My compassion and sympathy for Kel had all but disappeared because I was preoccupied with the loss of my outlet, Caring Bridge. Even though my CB writing was about Kelly and melanoma, it was my personal time to step away and gather my thoughts. Kelly wanted to be free of my overly informative posts, and I needed a place to write about it. I wanted another powerful venue where I could reunite the positive forces that had been left.

I decided to focus my energies on me and abandon my controlling nature. Juicing continued because I believed in the benefits, but Kelly decided if I drank it alone. He continually complained about the quantity of pills he had to take; therefore, he frequently skipped his vitamins. His vitamin container remained empty until he filled it himself or asked me to do it. I tried to cease nagging and judging while turning a blind eye, but it felt like we were heading for a crash. Mutual support was vacant as we expelled our emotions through sarcasm, insults, and anger.

Did we have any control? Anything and everything within our being was under our authority, but we neglected to look inward.

## Thursday, July 7, 2011

When Kel spoke, he was Dr. Jekyll, but my actions turned him into Mr. Hyde. I wasn't sure what would upset him, so I tried to remain silent and focus on our drive to the Mayo Clinic. Like a baited statement, Kelly told me if his strength didn't improve, he was going to quit his job. I sat quietly and processed the words that just caused my heart to plummet. How long had I been in the dark? What wasn't he telling me?

Days before I stopped writing in CB, Kel implied everything I wrote was a lie. My writings were based upon what Kel shared and what I saw. I now know the big picture wasn't as it seemed; Kelly was afraid I'd write about everything he shared. His fears were justified; after all, so much of his life had already been shared. Originally I felt like Kel kept me in the dark, but I realized he was protecting himself until he felt safe.

His vitamin container was empty; would he fill it? I planned to juice; would he drink it? In order to help, I had to follow. Clarity!

## Friday, July 8, 2011

Conversations returned understanding while love reclaimed its priority status. Kel tweaked my nipples (which I despised) but he did it so quickly that I flailed my arms around like a girl. I giggled, and we kissed. This was an innocent, playful encounter that had healing attributes. Then Kel showed me his left hand agility. His right and left wrist movements were comparable, and we were both very proud. I felt this accomplishment would lift CB readers' spirits and rekindle positive momentum. Jokingly, I offered to write something, and he rolled his eyes, scoffed, and told me no.

Three unexpected gifts were proof that positive forces were welcomed and finding us. A board, a book, and CDs were about to change my life forever. While confiding in my sister, I shared my anxieties and fears. She told me about her vision board and helped me create my own. During one of our Mayo trips, Kelly's sister gave me a book called *The Law of Attraction.* She read this book after being diagnosed with MS and thought the subject matter might inspire me. Kelly received the third gift from a woman who had read his Caring Bridge site, but whom he had never previously met. *The Secret* was a CD set, and listening to it helped her through a tough time. She felt it could help him. It wasn't until weeks later I learned these gifts were intertwined; each came from the same ancient philosophy and played off one another. Unknowingly, some of their teachings had been part of my belief and were being practiced during this journey. Our lives were full of progression and growth as we became aware and conscious.

## Saturday, July 9, 2011

Kelly's mood swung like a pendulum, and it was hard to track and gauge. He continued talking badly about people, going to places he once avoided. Kelly used to reprimand me, "If you can't say anything nice ..."

While Kel placed recently purchased lawn ornaments throughout our yard, he told me he wanted to feel he contributed to the outside décor as well. Pride emitted from him and sadness overcame me because I knew he was questioning if this would be his last summer. When he finished outside, he moved indoors and cleaned. Apparently I wasn't doing enough because he ridiculed my efforts. As Kel walked to the kitchen, he admitted he forgot to take his chemo pill—not once, but twice. I started to say, "What will it take ..." and before I could finish my sentence, he accused me of nagging. I rephrased and started again, "What reminder can we come up with so that you will remember to take them?" He came up with solutions, but I wasn't sure if he utilized any. Reluctantly, I continued to follow his lead.

Writing positives dismantled the negatives, potentially eradicating them forever; therefore, I wrote, "How did you forget to take your chemo pill? Do you want to live? Do you want to die? Do you even care?" Then I wrote my acceptance proposal: "Allow Kel to find a system that works for him so he can successfully complete his daily responsibilities and further his healing process! Taking meds and vitamins was new to his regime he is adapting." Words evoke perspective.

I wanted to capture and bottle the pride that filled the room during the drag show. When we learned the drag community wanted to honor Kelly with a benefit show, I began picturing an evening filled with family, friends, and love. From near and far, our loved ones overflowed the room with their support. Kel once took the stage with many of the performing queens and kings and was always the most beloved performer and a crowd favorite. We were overwhelmed by the attendance and the energy that permeated. If melanoma fed on negativity and fear, it was being obliterated at the show. Laughter was continuous, and love filled our lives. Tears freely flowed down Kelly's cheeks, and similar emotions were released by all who stood near. I was proud Kel exhibited such courage and strength.

Several Caring Bridge readers were impacted when my updates ceased. During the drag show, I was approached by many who

said they felt out of touch, and their lack of knowledge had a profound effect on the energy they were putting forth. I wanted Kelly to remain in the forefront of everyone's minds because I believed all of us were part of his healing process. A new venue was needed in order to reunite the positive forces that had been displaced.

## Sunday, July 10, 2011

Unless we wanted to be put on ice for an indefinite amount of time while scientists discovered a way to make us immortal, we knew we had an expiration date. I predictably responded, "Very good," or, "Great," when I was asked how Kel was doing. I should have said, "He is living!" Kel embodied life, and happiness was his objective. During the drag show, Kelly said, "I am going to beat this. I will be one of those who gets to share my story." He made the statement to several people throughout the evening, and every time, he appeared to believe it even more. Kelly's everyday surroundings were like a giant invisible hug: protecting, loving, encouraging, and filling him with hope. From day one, we entered our relationship, knowing mortality would force us to go our separate ways, but never predicting when.

## Monday, July 11, 2011

The study coordinator was called and informed Kel had forgotten to take his pill. He was told to permanently skip any forgotten dose. Any what-ifs were left behind as if that pill had little bearing on the big picture. I became confident there was a positive reason why he forgot to take them; time would bring the answer. Kel began to take vitamins again, so I took it upon myself to fill his pill case, but allowed him to take them as he saw fit. I juiced; he drank it. I made dinner, which included broccoli; he ate it. I continued to follow his lead while making healthier choices for me.

Work stress was frequently discussed at home. Kel told me he had been trying to do a full-time job while working part-time hours and it was becoming too much. When he was asked to do more, he refused and explained why. I felt he was justified, but he felt guilty. Kelly's views on Caring Bridge were unchanged, but I wondered if work stress would have decreased if CB updates hadn't ceased.

We watched another episode of the television series about cancer. The main character met a woman who had recently been accepted into a clinical study. The woman handed her guardian angel good luck coin to the main character and advised her to ask her doctor if she could be part of the study. Kel looked at me and said, "One of those angel coins was lying on my desk last week." He had no idea where it came from, but he assumed a coworker placed it there. Maybe little and big signs were lost upon others, but no matter their size, inspiring happenings continuously occurred. We were more aware than ever before.

## Tuesday, July 12, 2011

When Kel arrived home from work, he looked exhausted. After a brief nap, he shared the day's stresses and contemplated whether or not he would be able to continue working. I felt patient as Kel released tension from within. Trying to be encouraging, I reminded him his return to full-time status was over three weeks away. He said, "You just don't understand how tired I am. I wouldn't be able to work like this. I'm not sure I will be able to handle forty hours." I listened and thought about the other choices he had but wasn't seeing. Remaining silent, I wondered if one of the teachings I had learned was true: "Wishing your good health will make it so."

When my father had colon cancer, I believe he focused on getting better so he could continue life with his wife and kids. A 15 percent chance of survival turned into more than twenty years of living. I was finding truth in the words I was hearing. In order to heal, you must focus on a healthy you: focus on a healthy you as if that is who you are. The question I never asked was "When do you see yourself being healed?" It felt like a reasonable question. My personal goal for Kel's good health was Easter: rebirth. I hoped Kel had his own timeframe, and much sooner than mine.

Chemo caused an increase in phlegm, and Kel had begun coughing up blood-filled blobs. He was able to pick tiny clots (for lack of a better term) from his nose. He blew out a large one, and it burst within the tissue. I was afraid of what I saw because there was so much blood. It was a side effect, and we acknowledged it positively: he was getting rid of crap within and it would help him feel better. We viewed the phlegm blobs as a way of ridding his body of tumors. Whatever Kel believed came true. Science could say it wasn't so because science wasn't (and had never been) based upon thought. His body was his temple, and what wasn't curable from the outside was curable from the inside: the power of self. Science is based upon fact, and therefore has the inability to prove or disprove this. Placebos work; husbands are having some of the same pregnancy symptoms as their wives. There are rational explanations. When an answer satisfies its listener, there lies the explanation he believes is rational. I believed Kel had the greatest power to heal himself; it was within. Can one ever get better if he thinks it is impossible to achieve? Positive thought has a much more valuable role in the life of the living than people realize or utilize.

## Wednesday, July 13, 2011

Vitamins were skipped in the morning but taken after work. I juiced, and he liked it. We did yard work before taking Chaos for a walk. Our time together was ordinary, and I assumed this was what Kelly had wanted all along.

Our close friends and family members were continually inquiring about the lack of Caring Bridge updates. There was a need to keep everyone informed and positive forces going, but Kel didn't have time (or make time) to do so. My concern for Kel's health had taken a backseat to letting him live, and he was right when he said, "This will be good for you." My updates were driving a wedge between us, and the only way for us to reconnect was through my CB separation. I loved Kel so much, I was governing his life as if it were mine.

## Thursday, July 14, 2011

Kel had been awake since 5:00 a.m. because of pains and stiffening. Since he questioned if they were caused by dehydration, he drank 16 oz of water. In order to maintain energy at work, Kel had increased his caffeine intake, but he wasn't drinking enough water and old pains were resurfacing. I asked him how much he had been drinking, and he said, "I tried thinking of how much water I had and I don't think it was enough, so that is why I forced 16 oz." It felt like we were repeating history. He was aware lack of water could cause cramping, stiffening, and many other things, but staying hydrated needed a plan and action.

When I got home from work, Kel was talking on the phone. His demeanor was bubbly and upbeat ... until he hung up. While telling me about his busy day, he slowly spiraled into negativity. He had an unusually light workload but it still wiped him out, causing him to worry about his full-time return. Kel recited the things he was unable to do rather than being grateful for the things he could. When he spoke with his friend, he was happy-go-lucky, but when he talked to me, his life sucked and woe was him. It wasn't fair. I looked at him and said, "How am I supposed to understand what you are going through when you aren't telling me what's going on? Has your life sucked that bad the last three weeks?" Kel felt like he was cheating work because he often had to sit down and catch his breath. He made multiple negative statements about his own job performance, but they were only his assumptions. After every one of my suggestions, he explained he couldn't do it and told me I just didn't understand what he was feeling. Then he told me, "Don't be surprised if I quit my job." When he went back part-time, his belief was "I can do this. I am ready for this." His mind-set turned into, "I haven't been able to work thirty hours. I can barely work twenty-five hours. When I go back full-time, I'll have to work split days and I won't be able to handle that." Kel was carrying stress brought on by his own thoughts, and he became fixated on how he would fail and let others down. For every negative I had a positive, and yet they were received poorly. Kel walked away and sought refuge in his car. Day in and day out, he added stress upon himself, and he finally arrived at a crossroads!

Kelly mocked me when I talked about the little engine that could. There was truth in the message, and he wasn't ready to be reminded of it. When he wanted to go back to work, I thought he was crazy, but he was ready and he thought he could ... and he did it. Every decision made should be one we believe will impact us in a positive way.

The Caring Bridge site became a powerful source of positive vibes and energy, and when the updates were halted, so was the connection among its readers. So I created my own internet blogging site. While giving me a voice, the intent was to reestablish the unity that had been misplaced. I believed the only way to gain perspective was to hear the perspectives of others, and this created that opportunity.

## Friday, July 15, 2011

Weeks earlier, I was feeding my face with cookies while encouraging Kel to eat healthier. He looked at me and said, "You sit there eating that shit and you nag me about what I eat. How is that fair?" It wasn't fair, but his question made me analyze our actions. When the first clinical study scans came back with promising results, I expected Kel to build upon the success. Days after that appointment, Kelly consciously altered his daily regimen by omitting juicing and vitamins. Instead, they became an occasional daily supplement, and I wondered why these positive healthy choices were reduced. Maybe it was unrelated, but his pain resurfaced. Whenever Kel experienced pain, my first inquiry was always what he had to eat and drink. It was the simplest way for me to remain proactive and determine if certain items affected his pain.

Our bodies ... how well did we know and understand them? Doctors told us to exercise, eat fruits and veggies, and drink plenty of water; these suggestions were based upon experience and knowledge. How much of what they said did we hear? Did we listen? Avoiding foods that triggered my allergies was a no-brainer; the side effects weren't worth a satisfied craving. Every ingested food had an effect, but was it positive or negative? When eating, we turned a blind eye to many unhealthy foods and then we would complain about how they made us feel. Eating certain meals made us lethargic and bogged us down, but were we aware when foods fueled and energized us? Acknowledging the effects of food should have made cravings take a backseat to a potentially healthier, happier life, but that was seldom the case.

If Kel ate healthy, drank tons of water, got adequate exercise, followed directions, treated his body like a temple, but still felt like shit, I would have expected him to bitch, whine, and complain. I promised myself the next time I felt like shit, I would use a mirror to reflect back and acknowledge what I did or didn't do for myself.

## Saturday, July 16, 2011

I uttered—more like screamed—"I can't wait until this year is over." Two thousand eleven forced invisible hands into my subconscious. The only thing that felt consistent was support. It was the one constant I continually relied on and looked to. With my heart and soul, it was the one constant I tried to offer Kelly every freakin' day. How was I doing? I was less than average in effectiveness. I tried to avoid asking myself *why* questions, but I wondered, "Why is it so difficult for me to be the perfect supporter and partner?" The answer was obvious: perfection was unachievable. I could only offer what felt right and accept any pains that may have come along with my judgments and decisions. When my decisions sucked, the effects were drastic, but I learned from them. The moment decisions became too difficult, I'd reflect back to when I admitted I was gay. It was the most difficult and life-altering decision I would and will ever make, and by far my greatest accomplishment.

Years ago, when I was going through therapy, I gained tools and used them frequently. As I drove to my appointments, I would vow not to talk about certain painful topics because I was tired of crying over them. Every freakin' time I sat on the therapist's couch, I would talk about the shit I wanted to avoid and then leave feeling relieved and free from some bad shit. The things I wanted to avoid were the things I needed to face head-on because it was my way out of my own personal hell. I knew the road I wanted to walk, but sometimes I needed help staying on the path. If I felt the elephant in the room was in my way, I was going to greet the elephant and move forward. I wanted Kelly to introduce me to his elephants so we could move them off his path. It was difficult knowing they were there and I was unable to push them out of his way.

## Sunday, July 17, 2011

A familiar pain had resurfaced and the answer to why would have been a speculation; even doctors were reduced to an educated guess. I felt so far removed from Kel's internal truths, I was left with my uninformed thoughts. I tried to understand what was taking place within, but that was a feat better suited for a psychic. Our spirits lifted when positive energies surrounded us, so thinking, speaking, and infusing positive energy became my plan of action. I hoped to enhance Kel's internal belief system, and if his system was down, I wanted to assist in getting it up and running. My perfect incorporation was a work in progress and a first-time effort. A thought, belief, and a plan—wasn't that how every miracle began?

# Friday, July 22, 2011

Kelly entered his fourth phase of chemo, and I was supporting him the way I thought I'd want to be supported. It came naturally, but I started to lose control when I tried to gain it. The moment cancer entered our lives its affects were so vast that our new normalcy became the craziness surrounding the word. Well into the sixth month, much of the storm had settled, but the clouds still hovered, and every now and then I got poured on. Undesirable personal characteristics emerged and were in need of change. The control freak within had to be left at the door, and I had to relearn effective ways to shower Kel with support.

**Kelly sent this e-mail on the twenty-second:**

*In all honesty, the last few weeks have been some of the most difficult. I truly feel I'm trying my best to manage my illness, manage my relationship, and, of course, keep my job. At points, it feels like it is all too much, but just when I'm almost ready to give up, something positive happens. Caring Bridge started out being an excellent way to get the word out, but I felt toward the end it was turning more into a story and one that I didn't always agree with (the writings were Joe's thoughts of me and how he felt I was doing). There are no doubts that better days lie ahead, and now comes the wait to see if my work will accept me working thirty-two hours per week until further notice (this is the most I feel I can handle at this time). Whatever is decided, I have prepared myself, and only time will tell.*

# Chapter Nine

## Kelly and Joe

### Saturday, July 23, 2011

*Hey, everyone,*

*I said, "Hey everyone!" Tap! Tap! I know it has been a while!*

*Well it has been several weeks since the last post; however, I want you all to know that you really haven't missed much. Work is going fairly well; however, I still find myself crashing for a few hours at the end of the work day. This of course doesn't allow much family time during the work week, but Joe and Chaos have been wonderful, and let's face it, most of us need to work to pay our bills.*

*Moving on ... Last week was a challenging one that caused me to miss two days of work. One of my lung tumors acted up, applying continuous pain and only allowing me to take small breaths. This pain was something familiar to me as it had happened twice before (and X-rays were taken to eliminate the possibility of a blood clot). The doctors said to control it with my pain meds and adjust them as necessary. In the past, the pain lasted about three days; unfortunately, this time it was just under five. I'm happy to be writing this now with very minimal discomfort.*

*Blood work was completed this past Thursday, and the only concern that came from it was that my blood platelet count was low. Mine was 93 when average is 150–450. What this basically means is that my body would have a hard time stopping blood or creating a scab in the event I got cut. Because of the count, it was determined that my chemo pill assigned through the study will only be taken three days per week versus five.*

*As always,*

*We greatly appreciate all your support!*

*Kelly*

*P.S. Those with sharp items, stay away!*

## Tuesday, July 26, 2011

Most days were filled with obligations, requirements, and responsibilities, so after taking Chaos for a walk, I said, "I think we should sit on the deck." It was a breezy, cool evening, and we were grateful for everything while doing nothing. Sitting side by side, Kel dozed and I found the moment rich in every way. We were listening to the wind blow through the leaves, the hum of traffic, wind chimes singing while dancing, ships' horns announcing their arrival and the Canal Lift Bridge answering back with two blows, and bats flying through the night sky.

Every moment was free to enjoy. It was a priceless package deserving of a deep breath and a sigh. We were blessed with life.

The day was a success and our night was calm. Tomorrow was always an empty page waiting to be written.

## Thursday, July 28, 2011

A wise person, Kelly, told me to stop taking the lead. My intent was always for the better, but the question was, for whom? There were things that weren't mine to govern, but I still tried. I made his survival my fight and ended up feeling defeated when I was rejected. The Serenity Prayer should have been tattooed on my pointer finger because I needed a reminder to stop imposing what I thought was best. I needed to share without forcing my beliefs while allowing Kelly time to weigh their pros and cons. My desperation for our continued togetherness was fueled by fear, but ruled by love.

**Kel sent this e-mail on the twenty-ninth:**

*I find myself having more and more fatigue issues, but it's probably from still getting used to being back at work. Speaking of work, today started out crazy! I actually kicked an employee out of my office. Boy, did it feel good! If anything, having cancer is not going to let my staff push my buttons. Other news, I finally graduated from my physical therapy, and it feels good to get that behind me. Anyway, I'm getting winded! Sending hugs and love!*

# Sunday, July 31, 2011

During three separate occasions in three months, Kel said, "I feel really, really good. The pain is gone and I want this to last forever." The calm and peaceful quality of his voice was sweet and true. I had never verbalized my inner peace or happiness the way Kel expressed these moments to me. It was a familiar, yet seldom felt, perfect moment. We assessed everything leading up to this pain-free occasion in hopes of discovering the formula. I wanted to bottle his freedom from pain so I could give it to him again and again.

Could it be Kel surrendered his daily expectations and allowed the moments to be? Was it possible to have a perfect moment any time he wished? It didn't really matter because we were living every minute and cherishing the perfect ones.

# Thursday, August 4, 2011

*Good evening!*

*Before I forget, last Friday I graduated from my physical therapy. It sure is nice to have full movement and strength back in my left hand! Boy does one take for granted the use of it! Moving on, today was another eventful day in Rochester, where I received two and a half hours of chemo. Blah! But the wonderful news: shortly into my session, my study coordinator stopped in with a big smile. She informed us that all my blood counts were way up. This, of course, put smiles on our faces, but I think she was looking for a bit more. She then continued to inform us that it was the fifteenth day into my cycle and this is when my counts have always been very low and at their worst. She looked directly at me and said, "Kelly this is really, really good news!" This of course made us more responsive, and it was a super day from there forward.*

*Well, I'm done with appointments until Wednesday the seventeenth, when my tumors will be measured and discussed with us on the eighteenth. Chances are you won't hear anything from me until then, but know I'm still keeping my spirits high!*

*Sending love and appreciation to you all,*

*Kelly*

*P.S. My eight-and-a-half-hour work days have thus far been going excellent.*

## Thursday, August 4, 2011

Name the most important thing you want in your life, from your life. Does bitching about work, a friend, a driver, etc. fulfill that importance? Does a lack of positivity and an abundance of dreadful negativity sum up your life? Worry warts, busy bodies, negative Nellys, Debby downers, positive thinkers, free spirits—I was placing everyone in a category deserving of their reaction to Kel's status. When I looked at Kel, he was bright, with his usual sparkle in his eyes. He was going through horrible shit and yet his brilliance still shined. I was sorry he had to live with any of this hell, but I refused to live in fear and doubt. We lived in light. We may have had limitations, but Kel was an extension of my life, with zero limitations. Happy moments were remembered while we focused on the future waiting to be created. We were living life.

## Saturday, August 6, 2011

Kel and I used to live for weekends, and we were missing our days of fun, fun, fun. We missed our gatherings, loud music, and social drinking, but we were also thirsty for irresponsibility and freedom. We went out for the evening, and though my internal energy wanted to be present, my outward enthusiasm was lacking. There were plenty of opportunities to create laughter and chatter, but I just wanted to absorb the surroundings without having to communicate. Within minutes of our arrival, the main topic became melanoma. Kel shared his story while offering encouragement, hope, and wisdom. During this time, our friend told us he learned about his melanoma status two days after Kelly's diagnosis. Our friend's treatment consisted of its removal and follow-up doctor's visits every four months— different scenarios for different people. Kelly took us back to the first day that "You have melanoma" was uttered, and as he spoke about the early days, it felt like the air was sucked from my lungs. Memory caused emotional pains, and I was stuck in the past, crippled in the present, and the future lacked purpose. Reliving Kelly's cancer journey was neutralizing my energy needed to propel me forward. After further listening, I realized Kel was proudly sharing his story, and I knew our past wasn't going to keep us from the tomorrow we planned to attend. When we headed home, Kelly told me he had a good time.

## Monday, August 8, 2011

Was there ever a break from it? Within five minutes of entering my first store for work, I was engaged in a conversation about

Kel and his status. When people asked for updates, I felt there was a genuine concern for both of us, but sometimes I wanted to be free from it all. Fortunately, sometimes when I slept, I was free. Besides Kel, I assumed I was the most consumed by our circumstances, and rightfully so. Our relationship had always been built upon growing together, and we continued to do so—the same journey with individual experiences.

## Friday, August 12, 2011

In order to avoid risks, we altered our friend-filled summer camping weekend and relocated. Cabin quarters replaced tents and made for a much more accommodating way to overcome obstacles. However, pain was an unpredictable pest and infested Kel a few times, changing the course of the weekend but certainly not overtaking it. As each painful bout was passed, moments of relief were had by all. Our getaway was different, but friends proved to be one of our many constant fortunes.

**Our traditional yearly camping group:**
**Tara Lien, Kelly, Me, Julie Dahl, and Spencer Erkkila.**

Joe Peterson

I had spent months sharing myself, absorbing things around me, trying to translate what it all meant, and foreseeing what was ahead. When times were difficult, writing helped me cope. When times were going great, writing it down made it last. Our future was unknown, but writing helped me feel better prepared for it because I was more appreciative of the present. An internal journey is very lonely, so I went external as often as I was surrounded by loving individuals. Sharing released more and more feelings of loneliness, and as I spoke, I felt less isolated.

## Sunday, August 14, 2011

When Kel met with radiology, he was informed of the potential side effects from radiation. The list was lengthy but a necessary tradeoff for life. Precautions were taken to protect surrounding vulnerable areas. I was disappointed because the physical effects were becoming more severe than we were informed, but life remained the focal point.

One week before our annual camping weekend, Kel was in excruciating pain and discovered a white thing protruding from his gum. To my uneducated eye, it looked like an ulcer; he had several during radiation and it looked like those. Using one of his dental tools, he scraped and picked the surface. It was hard like a tooth, and an internet search convinced us it was a bone spur. He was in horrible pain during our camping trip until he picked out the fragment with his fingernail. His finger was bloody, the spur was out, and he was finally getting a break from pain.

A dentist confirmed the extraction was part of a tooth and most likely a remnant from a previous procedure. Since Kel was free from pain, no further investigating was done. Days had passed before Kelly discovered another fragment, this one on the opposite side of his mouth. We made an appointment with a Mayo Clinic dentist, and he confirmed they were in fact tooth fragments. Because of radiation, Kel's teeth were crumbling at the root, and the pieces were making their way out through his gums. The man who caught my attention with his smile was not only battling cancer, his beautiful teeth were falling apart. Kel extracted three more fragments, and each caused him much pain until they were dislodged.

## Tuesday, August 16, 2011

There were bound to be changes and a shift in responsibilities, but this was the first time I felt aware of the health crisis. Kel was back at work and all his energy was zapped before returning home. Dinner together was a luxury that rarely happened, and our nightly walks were dictated by his sleeping needs. Our ordinary old habits had been broken by circumstances and necessities. I wanted quality time with Kelly, but I had to learn to appreciate every moment we were near one another.

## Thursday, August 18, 2011

The morning was spent in Rochester, and the second set of scans had not gone as we had hoped. In the evening and back at home, Kel was trying to get his pain under control and get as much rest as possible. Exhaustion had control over both of us. Before heading to work, I kissed Kel as he lay in bed, preparing to write in CB. I tried calling him throughout the evening with zero success. I called a family member to see if Kelly had posted an update. He hadn't. I began to panic because when I kissed him, his laptop had been open and ready for him to type. What was going on? I rushed through my workload, hurried home, and ran into our bedroom. My fears were side by side with a potential reality: I thought I had lost him. Kelly's head was resting on our headboard, and the wrought iron coiling left a deep red indent. It felt like I was prying his head from adhesive as I yelled and shook him awake. After I calmed down and Kel became more alert, he said, "My head hurts." Kel literally passed out the moment I went to work, and not only was I happy that he got some sleep, I was grateful I had more time with him.

## Friday, August 19, 2011

*This past week has been a big challenge because of continuous spiking pains and fatigue. Luckily I had appointments at the Mayo so I could discuss it with them.*

*Wednesday Afternoon: CT scan at the Mayo. Wait till Thursday for results.*

*Thursday Morning: Appointment with my oncologist to discuss scan results and go over meds, pain, etc.*

*I started by informing the doctor about my recent pain levels, which have been unbearable (spiking to ten regularly), along with breathing problems. The doctor stated he wasn't surprised by what I had told him, because of the scan results. It showed that the tumors have grown in my chest/lungs and stomach, thus causing the pain and breathing issues. There are also tumors that have shrunk, but since other tumors grew more than 20 percent since treatment began, they will not keep me in the clinical study; so I was told I was being removed. We were quite sad to hear this but know that something else is out there for me. We next wondered what was going to happen as I normally would have received chemo that day. Before I could ask the question, the doctor informed us my blood platelet levels were very low so I couldn't receive any type of chemo for another week. This will also give them time to set up a new plan of action and get the drug information sent for preapproval by insurance.*

*By now, many of you have heard of all the new wonderful melanoma treatments, drugs, etc. Please be advised that there are numerous types of melanoma and unfortunately mine is not treatable by "those" drugs. I have "garden variety," meaning that I don't have a specific strain to attack (I have many). The recent news has mainly focused around those having a B-Raff melanoma, which is generally less than 50 percent diagnosed. My doctor is very progressive and up on all the new drugs, so he clarifies these things. Otherwise he would need to answer to Joe. Ha!*

*Before leaving, I asked for life length statistics based on my current visit, and the news I was given isn't something anyone wants to hear (it is basically the same as before). However, I will continue to stay positive and hold on to the doctor's words: "I hope I'm wrong."*

**This was an e-mail conversation between my family member and Kelly on the nineteenth:**

Family Member: *Today's news wasn't ideal ... or was it? Maybe the time you spent in the study was just a stepping stone, a building block to get you strong and ready for this direction of healing. Are you ready? I ask because I've heard you say on many occasions that you are fighting, that you will be the one who beats this, that you will be the one to tell your story to help others beat this. You say it with such strength and conviction, and we all believe those words you say—in fact we cling to them ... but do you? If you could tell your story today, what would you say? How would you describe how you fought, how you won? Your words need to match how you react because if they don't work together, they are simply not working. Fight, Kel, fight with every breath you take, fight with every bone in your body, fight with every hair on your head (no matter how short), and above all, fight with the belief that you can beat this. People do, you know! You are never too weak to be internally strong! These are your words, Kel: "Cancer is not me." I am not ready to throw in the towel, nor is anyone else, so grab hold and take your life back!*

**Kel:** *Thanks so much for the reminder of my words! Yes, this past week has been hell, and I will admit that throwing in the towel was on my mind. I have enjoyed returning to work; however, I know since going back, my quality of life has changed completely.*

Unable to continue writing, Kelly's brief response was followed with a phone call to the recipient. At the time, he was flooded with emotion and asked me to express his gratitude for her direct approach. My family member held Kelly accountable, and he thanked her for treating him the same way she would have treated me. During the phone conversation, Kelly became aware he was much more than my partner— he was family.

# Friday, August 26, 2011: The Prayer

We were about to be surrounded by more strength and power than ever before. Seeking information on the internet about our aunt who was a nun in St. Scholastica's Monastery in Duluth, Minnesota, my sister came across "Submit a Prayer." She didn't find much written about our aunt, but it felt like she found exactly what she was meant to. She submitted a prayer for Kelly.

The response:

*The Sisters are happy to pray for Kelly as he fights this cancer, and for you. Please keep us in your prayers as well.*
*May God's peace and grace be with you both,*
*The Sisters of St. Scholastica Monastery*

*"I pray for good health to return to Kelly Boedigheimer. That he finds faith and the inner strength to beat melanoma and is able to share his journey of success with others in need."*

# Thursday, September 1, 2011

*To Work or Not to Work.*

*Well since my last post, my pain has definitely gotten much better (hip, hip hurray!) and because of this, I've actually been able to sit and analyze my current quality of life.*

*After speaking with my doctor along with thinking about what I have accomplished since returning to work, I came to the conclusion that I hated my life! The routine of continuously working, sleeping, receiving treatment, and eating is not the lifestyle I want. With this said, it was a no-brainer that it was time to give notice and leave Black Bear (last day: September 6).*

*I can't believe I'm saying this, and I will blame the meds down the road, but …*

*Joe was right!*

*All my positive energy was being used at work while I regularly came home overtired and cranky, taking it out on him and Chaos. Even though I love my job and will miss it terribly, I look forward to spending more time with my family without being tired.*

*Speaking of tired, I think this is enough for now.*

*Thank you all for your continued support!*

*Kelly*

**Kelly sent this brief e-mail on September second:**

*My biggest fear about this weekend is ensuring no one hugs me too hard, as it upsets my tumors, like old people. Ha! I have weak spots on my body that will remind me at a later point that I overdid it (the story of my life).*

## Saturday, September 3, 2011

No expectations, no disappointments … have truer words ever been spoken? Kel and I were heading into our seventh month of events, plans, and celebrations that had to be altered to some degree. It was Pride weekend in Duluth, Minnesota, and our kick-off to month seven. Party, party, party was replaced with sleep (for Kel) and writing (by me).

As I thought about our friends celebrating and having a great time, I felt like I was missing the social networking. My memories were of Pride parties, and my emotions were peaked by our absence. Then I watched Kel and Chaos, both sleeping on the couch. Chaos opened one eye and caught me staring, while Kel readjusted and appeared peaceful. My desire to be anywhere else faded as a smile formed. It wasn't a party, but I was surrounded by love. Special moments couldn't be created or assured; they happened without effort or control.

## Sunday, September 4, 2011

Kelly continued a tradition he had been part of for many years: greeting passengers for Gay Pride's Fruit Float, a three-hour boat party on Lake Superior. I was there in the now, aware everything was relevant to the present. Comparisons to the past could wait until a later date. Sunday met every expectation ... there were none! Several individuals had come to know and appreciate Kel, and their love and support for him was obvious. Before stepping aboard, I hugged Kelly and whispered into his ear, "Let the love and support from all of these people help shatter those fucking tumors inside!"

## Tuesday, September 6, 2011

This was Kelly's last day of work. His place of employment threw him a retirement party and honored his twenty years of service. Hundreds of well-wishers attended, and it became very obvious to me that Kel was respected and loved and was going to be missed. Socializing exhausted him, and I could sense he was experiencing some pain, so we left his party a bit early. Once again, my partner touched more lives than I was ever made aware of, and I felt blessed and privileged that he chose to be with me.

## Thursday, September 8, 2011

Melanoma was a bitch that produced pain and suffering. Radiation, chemo, and painkillers were bastards that caused nasty side effects. The tumors wreaked havoc, procedures used to fight tumors wreaked havoc, and painkillers were used to mask the havoc being wreaked. It was a vicious cycle. It was a lose-lose-lose situation, and there was only one way out of this hell: Kel had to live. Kelly was flooded with problems, but he never let the current wash him away.

## Sleep

Kelly and I continually tried to overcome difficulties and obstacles faced during sleep: changing positions or locations, adding or removing pillows, lying flat or sleeping upright. Even if Kel found comfort and slumber, I resisted, because monitoring his breathing and actions felt more important. Sleep-apnea-type symptoms, body jolts, and unexplained arm movements made it almost impossible for Kelly to reach a dream stage.

Anytime Kel fell asleep on the couch, his uncontrolled arm movements began. I felt the need to record his behavior in hopes of gaining perspective. I also wanted to see if Kelly could shed some light on his actions. While he viewed the recorded footage, Kel sobbed and cried out, "What is happening to me?" Had I known it would induce such a terrified reaction, I would have never shown him. All I could do was hug and comfort him as best I could.

I witnessed these strange arm movements for quite some time, but I resisted sharing it with anyone because it frightened me and I didn't want (or wasn't ready for) outside opinions. It didn't matter if Kelly was sitting upright or lying on his back, his arms would stretch out and hover as if each wrist was attached to a puppet string. Each arm floated freely (up and down) but in unison. As his consciousness returned, his arms would fall. I was smacked several times because I couldn't predict their landings, especially in bed, where it was dark. When I pulled down on his arms, I encountered an enigmatic force. I was unable to move his arms, and the resistance overpowered any amount of pressure I applied. Kel's power source was intimidating and unfamiliar to me. He was never able to offer any insight, but I had my own speculations.

## Thursday, September 22, 2011

My well-being was just as much of a concern to Kel as his own health, and it came as no surprise when he asked, "What would you do if I didn't wake up tomorrow? Have you thought about that?" I hated the fact that this question had plagued me for many months, but I would have hated myself more if I neglected to tell the truth. Of course I thought about it. I had been in situations that felt like his time was near. I hated the feeling that consumed me when this thought was present. I hated how afraid, scared, and alone it made me feel. Again, Kel asked, "What would you do?" I told Kel I thought about traveling to all of the places we talked about visiting but hadn't. I planned to continue doing things we did together because I refused to become tainted and jaded by life. I didn't want to avoid having his memory surround me, because he was part of my fortune.

## Friday, September 23, 2011

Kelly received chemo as planned, but his blood work revealed elevated enzyme levels, which was common if the cancer had spread or grown. Because of the elevated levels, his doctor made plans to have scans done three weeks earlier than previously forecasted. We had five days to ponder and prepare before his scheduled scans—five days for every prayer, well-wish, and positive thought to find Kel and nurture him back to good health.

## Monday, September 26, 2011

Like in the past, lack of sleep and pain meds were taking a toll on Kel. While I was working, I called him, and he sounded sad and exhausted. I knew the only place for me was at home, by his side. It was a beautiful fall day, and I was determined that we would go and be part of it. We embraced the outdoors and filled our lives with people, activities, and things we loved. Experiencing everything in our path, we were grateful for every moment. Hours of enjoyment were followed by hours of sleep, a deep snoring sleep. It was exactly what Kel needed and a sound I loved hearing.

I had always known that there was nothing more important to me than love. The more I was surrounded by love, the more I wanted to be surrounded by more of it. Maybe growing up in such a large family made me addicted to the affection or maybe it was a side effect of being loved and knowing I was loved. It didn't matter; Kelly and I were in love and life had purpose.

## Thursday, September 29, 2011

*I woke up with the usual aches and pains. After a shower and my meds, the pain became more tolerable. Twenty more minutes until the results are given regarding the cancer growth. I am going into this very positive. Even in the event that the tumors have grown, I have come to realize that balloons need to become bigger before they pop and become garbage!*

*Joe will give more details later in the day. Keep in mind the hours of travel we have.*

*Kelly*

Kel had experienced spiking pain throughout his body. He was unable to walk to his first appointment because leg spasms made him unstable and could have potentially knocked him down. We were told cancer releases toxins that can cause this pain, and the havoc can occur virtually anywhere. Kel's sweats had increased from once or twice a week to numerous times daily, just like a menopausal woman. We did whatever we could to combat and speed through this effect. We were both nervous to learn the scan results, but Kel's words of hope were examples of the way he approached life: positively!

Several individuals inquired about Kelly's scans, and while they were being taken, our loved ones intended to send positive energy his way. Most of us grew up hearing, "Ask and you shall receive." All we asked for were healthy scan results.

Unfortunately, Kel's scans verified the tumors had grown and spread. His blood work levels were slightly higher than the previous week, and he was on the verge of needing a blood transfusion. Continued chemo had a 50/50 chance of helping or hurting; it still wasn't a cure. Things went the opposite of what we had hoped, but the change did not leave us hopeless.

Several physicians were consulted, and their opinions were unanimous with how they would proceed; Kelly agreed. He decided to stop chemo. If new advancements arrived, they intended to reconnect with us and we would move forth, but until then, our Mayo trips had come to an end. Kel was advised to enter hospice, and upon hearing the word, we felt destitute. What we were told was that hospice was the best at controlling pain and making life as comfortable as possible for individuals. Kel's doctor would have recommended hospice two months earlier, but a person receiving chemo was not eligible. *What?* Because Kel was getting chemo treatments, he was not able to receive pain assistance from hospice? Apparently this was an insurance rule.

Since the beginning of our journey, we were made aware there was not a modern medical cure for melanoma. Knowing that fact didn't help me prepare for this day, but Kel was making several positive comments and sounded ready to take 100 percent control. It was 12:10 p.m. We were crying as we drove away from the Mayo Clinic. In awe and disbelief, I said, "Can you hear that?" I rolled the windows down and let the sound of spirited church bells flow through. On two other occasions, each representing a new chapter, those same bells chimed, but never so vibrantly. Another beginning was upon us.

# Friday, September 30, 2011

When we told Kel's family about his dismissal from the Mayo, they reacted with their best efforts at encouraging and supporting him: being matter-of-fact and emotionless. This was devastating news, and they were trying to be strong. After we left his family, I asked Kel for his thoughts regarding their reactions. His response: "I think they are so used to the ups and downs that things don't really affect them anymore." I knew this was not the case because I had had previous conversations with his family; there was hardly a dry-eyed moment when we spoke of Kel. I told Kelly about my personal experiences with his family in hopes of making him aware how affected they truly were. Kelly was always trying to be strong for everyone who loved him and often withheld his emotions. I knew he would come to understand his family's reaction. When I shared their emotional breakdowns, Kel released some of his own. Safe to say, we all felt helpless. It was difficult knowing what to do at this point.

Searching for a solution to his plague, Kel was alone with his decisions. Professional advice offered little optimism, and personal opinions were based upon belief without fact. I wanted to put forth perfection because that was all we had room for, and yet I knew that was impossible. When Kel spoke about his fears, pains, and cancer, I would attempt to turn his frown upside down. His truths broke my heart, and my defense was to offer him my well-intended suggestions. My tactics had stressed Kelly out on numerous occasions, and I started questioning if I was hurting more than helping. Neither of us liked this roller-coaster ride, but we were on it together until the end.

# Saturday, October 1, 2011

Like any balanced relationship, Kel and I had weak and strong moments. I was feeling weak, and Kel was comforting me as I processed my emotions. Kelly's hug had healing powers, but his pain was now restricting our embrace and we were left with a wish and a want: Kel wished his pain would stop, and I wanted to make it stop. Much of the day was spent by Kelly's side, but I was far away in my own thoughts. I felt an odd force within my own energy, and when negativity crept in, I felt surrounded by it. Humor brought laughter, which brought glimpses of happiness, but it couldn't stop my "poor me" attitude.

We drove to my parents' home in St. Paul, and several of my family members stopped by to see Kelly. While telling them about his Mayo Clinic discharge, his spirit appeared broken and he cried when saying, "I just feel like everyone has given up on me." Every eye was tear-filled as we expressed our belief in him. Kelly had faith in his medical team, and he depended on them to treat him. A poor transition between the Mayo Clinic and hospice caregivers left Kel feeling temporarily abandoned and alone. Once Kelly's feelings were expressed, his confidence began to surface. He continued telling my family he was excited for the chemo drugs to leave his system because he wanted to see what his own body could do.

In the evening, we attended our dear friend's daughter's wedding reception. Kel and I had been guests at many weddings, but we had never felt this comfortable or safe. Our security was directly impacted by the fact that the brother of the bride was also gay and accompanied by his partner. We celebrated a rite we didn't have the right to personally experience, yet our love was as pure. Nothing, not even cancer, could intercede as we proceeded as if it were our very own wedding. For our first and last wedding slow dance, we held one another tight and my tears landed upon his shoulder. Mortality was closing in, but our lives were blossoming.

## Monday, October 3, 2011

The most important place for me was by Kel's side; my mind was already there. My hope and optimism was present, but when I was told the person I loved was going to die, my emotional recovery was slow. Juggling life's responsibilities and being the partner I wanted to be for Kelly proved impossible, and something had to change.

I sought short-term disability and was dumbfounded by modern medicine and health insurance. Not once was I ashamed of the tears I shed or the emotions I expressed. Not once did I wish I could stifle my feelings or hide my fears. I felt sad, I felt scared, but I was sane enough to analyze my thoughts and write them down as I processed. I was sane enough to know the place I wanted to be was by Kel's side. Professionals had an idea of what would benefit me the most, and insurance had specific requirements that needed to be followed. What was my prescription? Even though there wasn't a pill to cure Kelly, there was a pill that could help me stop feeling and crying. I was placed on short-term disability, and my protocol was pills.

My biggest desire was being by Kel's side, and I knew it would be my greatest benefit. I didn't want to mask emotions; I wanted the freedom to cry so hard it took my breath away. My emotions peaked when I was away from Kel; my heart was at peace when I was near him.

## Tuesday, October 4, 2011

Kel and I had numerous talks. Every day brought laughter, and we were finding a groove that worked for us. Family walks were very much part of our daily regimen, and Chaos loved it. I was proud of Kelly. His attitude remained upbeat and positive as he processed and deduced ways to save his life. My place was at home, and my purpose was to support and encourage both of us. Together, we were a team.

# Chapter Ten

## Hospice

### Wednesday, October 5, 2011

As promised, hospice was going to assist Kel with pain, sleep, and his overall quality of life. When I asked about beneficial food choices, hospice representatives recited the same statement that had been repeated over and over throughout this journey: eat whatever you want. I grew up learning about the importance of good nutrition, yet when Kel was diagnosed, only one doctor encouraged the power of food. It was dire Kel kept weight on during his treatments, but sadly, those treatments tainted his taste buds and never offered a cure. If keeping weight on was a cure, I would have continuously baked for him. I believed professionals wanted Kelly to enjoy what he was eating, but that only convinced me they didn't believe he was going to survive.

Was there a facility that never formed judgment, where personal opinions weren't guided by previous experiences, a place that allowed the patient to live until he died? Too many individuals painted the picture for Kel when they should have allowed him to be the artist of his finest piece. Kelly owned his survival plan, and I was left remembering the only supportive doctor's words: "We have choices, we have options, and we have hope. The only things proven to help fight cancer are sleep, exercise, water, and a plant-based diet."

## Wednesday, October 5, 2011

The spoken word had quite an impact. Kel and I were called fag and queer, and those words hurt. We were given melanoma statistics, and those words caused fear. Every day, Kel and I would say, "I love you," and those words felt awesome. It didn't seem like anyone had the right to use words forewarning Kel about experiences he may or may not encounter, but they did. Many warnings and shared experiences were biased and placed upon Kel's current status. Was it necessary to share potential trauma he might endure? It may not have been the intent, but it seemed like every empty thought pocket was filled with negativity. I wanted to believe hospice was going to be a source of hope and offer Kelly quality of life care into recovery. Unfortunately, we heard, "Oh, honey, eventually you won't want to eat. Things will become more difficult and it may be necessary to be admitted." We were also told, "We try to supply you with as much information so there are no surprises." If hospice could offer Kelly a better quality of life, why did everything pertain to death?

I wanted to scream out to the world, "Cancer entered our lives and we have been living with challenges for nine months. Times have been difficult, and yet our love, hope, and support has grown stronger. Do you really think there is a need to tell us what we might experience? Let's work with the facts directly related to Kel and no other stats, no what-ifs, no probabilities, and help him live rather than prepare for death."

I didn't find comfort in ugly details that may or may not occur. I found stats to be distracting because they were a competing factor that was tainted. I believed diet was crucial at every point during Kelly's life and had the potential to save him. Expertise wasn't going to decide his outcome. A professional judgment may be the same for every person dealing with a similar situation, but I find that to be biased, without hope. Survival may not be possible for most, but there is always the miracle that walks away.

As hospice staff left our house, they were told our rules: we are here to live, and we expect you to help us. When entering our home, we want everyone present, thinking positive, and believing anything is possible.

## Thursday, October 6, 2011

Kel looked at me and said, "Can you believe this shit, Joey?" "No, I can't," was all I could muster before we hugged and cried.

Kelly was told to stop taking all of his prescription drugs and begin taking the medication supplied through hospice. I questioned the effects of stopping such high doses of painkillers but was assured the new medication would eliminate any withdrawal. Within hours, Kelly was experiencing familiar pains, and his discomfort worsened. The new pain blockers took up to twelve hours to become established within his system, and during that time, Kel had to endure what he feared most: pain. We were ready to reap some rewards, and we were confident that in hours, we would.

## Friday, October 7, 2011

During Kelly's medication conversion, I made an error and reported a lesser dose amount for one particular drug. Because his pain had gotten worse (under hospice care), Kel analyzed the drug conversions and discovered my mistake. Hospice immediately increased the med dose, which eventually offered some relief. We were impressed with their speed to action.

It was imperative we shared our outlook and the expectations we had so Kel would receive the best care possible. After we explained our wishes, the spiritual, social, and bereavement advisers made known their roles in Kel's care. We began to have faith in hospice's ability to assist our goals with living. Offering a source of comfort, our home health care nurse brought aroma therapy and informed us of other nontraditional practices available.

I was very proud of our travels, and we told caregiver after caregiver of our hope-filled journey. This puzzling life isn't what we would have chosen, but the pieces felt like they were falling into place. Every challenge came with personal growth—boy, how we had grown. While Kel napped, the scent of lavender blanketed his presence, and I envisioned his body, mind, and soul at peace.

## Sunday, October 9, 2011

Every day was full of life, but I couldn't remember a day that wasn't challenging. Long gone were the days of taking easy carefree moments for granted. Instead, we were praying and hoping a carefree moment would occur. Kelly brought so much life into my world, and I was grateful for every day he did.

Things were familiar rather than under control. It was extremely difficult for Kel to get past the daydream state, and he was starting to suffer from deprivation. Sleep issues accompanied every medication or dose change, and history seemed to be repeating itself. Kelly was exhibiting the same behaviors I witnessed during our Mayo travels: confusion, frustration, and agitation. Though Kel felt as if he had entered REM, he was continuously twitching and moving about. Frequently, he would startle himself awake and then utter statements pertaining to his daydream state. Kel often realized his disconnect, and together we would make light of the situation. It was a present reality and something we chuckled about as we hoped for his sound sleep.

Quicker than the flip of a switch, Kel was drifting in and out of consciousness as we drove to the park for our daily family walk. In his daydream state, he said, "Well, we can take the plastic things off of Chaos ourselves." I assumed Kelly was talking about Chaos's current health issue, but I didn't know what plastic things he was referring to. When I asked, "What plastic things are you talking about?" Kel's eyes were open but he was still in his daydream state.

Within a few seconds, Kel was alert, and he scoffed, "I was babbling. I thought Chaos was having his hair highlighted and we could remove the plastic wraps." We were either going to find humor in what transpired or deal with a sense of disbelief, denial, and sadness. Our anxiety, like the situation, was familiar, so we made jokes, laughed, and even shared the story with others. As long as we accepted what was, our lives had stablility.

# Monday, October 10, 2011

If Kelly had been forewarned about all of the pain he'd encountered during his lifetime, I'm not sure he would have believed he'd have the strength to persevere. Pain and sleep continued to be an issue, and I felt one was the cause for the other. Oxygen was used at night, but sleeping continued to be restless. Although the pain meds were increased, the effects were minimal. Because the medication switch hadn't lessened his pain, Kelly wished he was still on the painkillers that were prescribed at the Mayo.

As he laid himself on the living room floor, trying to distance himself from the pain that was spiking throughout his body, I sobbed uncontrollably. He was dealing with his own issues, and still he said, "Oh, Joey, come here and give me a hug." I positioned myself close to him, and he rolled onto his side. We hugged as best we could. I don't think I ever cried so hard. "We are going to get through this, Joey. We always do!" is what he told me. As he tried to comfort me, his own pain had a hold on him. He told me to help him sit so he could give me a better hug. I had him wrap his arms around my neck so I could lift him, and we hugged and kissed, and I sobbed. I told him how much better he had made my life, and he told me I had done the same for him.

I had been missing his hugs, his touch, and our connection, how real and loving it was. I yearned for more. I wanted more and I needed more. I felt all was right and safe when he hugged me. My fortune was an emotional, physical, and loving experience shared with Kel. As the fight for gay marriage raged on, our souls were already united and our love trumped hate.

## Tuesday, October 11, 2011

We waited for several hours before hospice had a room for Kel's admittance. Every minute that passed at home, I could see Kel's condition worsening, and we were distraught. We let out an audible sigh of relief as we drove to the hospital.

When the doctor examined Kel, he said, "The reason why we suggest that new patients check themselves into the hospital is so we can level out their medication. That way we can avoid situations like this." Upon hospice's first visit at our house, we made it perfectly clear our wishes were to have Kel at home; we were never advised to admit him for the initial medication conversion. Pain was Kel's greatest fear, and to get control of it, we would have done anything they suggested. The doctor apologized after he learned hospice staff neglected to inform us of this protocol. Even though we were assured the switch would go smoothly, tests proved Kelly's body had a bad reaction to one of the newly prescribed drugs. Kel's estimated hospital stay was four to five days.

His facial coloring indicated oxygen levels were extremely low, and blood tests verified the need for a transfusion. When his levels increased, Kel had energy that could challenge a child's. It appeared as if the worst had passed, but the doctor brought Kel's family and me to a private room. He told us Kelly's status was grim and he was not expecting him to make it through the night. Permission was asked for a DNR. I gave it. As startling as the doctor's information was, it was imperative I remembered everything Kel had overcome. I believed Kel would pull through and eventually return home with me. I had witnessed his strength and courage, and this was history repeating itself. Kelly was going to walk out of there.

Exhausted, sick, and in the care of others, he lay in his hospital bed, out of our home, out of my control. I was going out of my mind. I had the fortune of being able to stay within his room. The second bed was there, but it felt as if it were miles away from his. He seemed unaware of my location, but I needed to physically be by his side. For much of the last twelve years we had slept side by side. I needed that comfort and security again.

I grabbed two chairs and staggered them while topping them with pillows. My lower legs were on one chair, my right hip rested on another, and my upper body was on the side of Kel's bed, getting my head as close as possible to his. It was an ideal solution to an overwhelming need. I was able to whisper in his ear, reminding him of his power, strength, and energy. Consciously, he may have been unaware, but I believed that, subconsciously, he knew I was by his side and he listened to every word I whispered.

As each nurse entered, I would wake and watch as she cared for him. Their reactions to my sleeping arrangements were the least of my concerns. I was close to the person I loved. I was grateful intolerance and prejudices were void throughout the night. When I believed Kel had reached a peaceful state, I moved to the other bed for my own much-needed rest. Love transcended all!

## Wednesday, October 12, 2011

Kelly was on very high doses of drugs when he said, "I don't know who you are but you can love me anyways." Every time I told Kel, "I love you so much," I just prayed to hear it in return, telling myself hearing it once more would be all I'd ask. As soon as Kel repeated the words, I longed to hear them again. I could never hear those words enough, tell him enough, or have explained how much I loved him.

At 4:00 a.m., Kelly finally fell asleep, and at 6:00 a.m., I was writing. It had only been two hours of solid rest for Kel and the most relief and joy I had in days. He got more sleep in the hospital than the five previous nights combined. He was looking good, sleeping soundly, and had gotten past another obstacle. Love and support had been the driving force, and it was steering us to health and home.

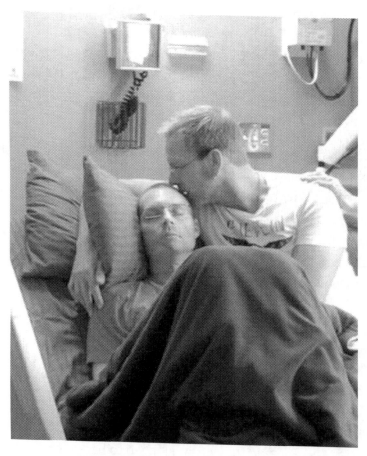

## Thursday, October 13, 2011

Life with Kel was a dream come true, but seeing him affected by disease was my nightmare. Whether caused by pain or medication, his body continuously twitched and jolted him awake. At 2:00 a.m., Kel was adamant we leave the hospital because he didn't want to withstand another night away from home. His desires were deterred by spiking pains that continued for the next three hours. Five medication increases were needed to stabilize him and offer comfort. While he slept, I whispered in his ear, "It's going to be a good day, Buck-A-Roo."

The doctor believed Kel would never go home or leave the hospital alive. This grim scenario was painted based upon previous cases. I felt his and the staff's doubt when I told them Kel would eventually be going home. They may have underrated Kelly's courage, strength, and determination, but we never underestimated the power of hope. For two days, their words did overpower my beliefs, and I was left sobbing uncontrollably for every visitor to see. I was reacting nothing like the person I had come to know and understand. I was lost in a reality that wasn't mine. My own reality began to resurface when my awareness and knowledge trumped the fear instilled by the hospital staff. Kelly said to me, "This is not my home. I don't want to die here. I don't know what this place is." Kel's wish was to be at home, and it remained my number one objective. We were going to make it a reality. To ensure the best possible transition home, a PICC (peripherally inserted central catheter) line was placed in his right arm. Medication was continuously pumped through this line, and if pain spiked, Kel administered an extra dose by the push of a button. I felt confident that home would welcome health ... for both of us.

Kelly often planned for worst-case scenarios, but he lived and lived large, turning negatives into positives. He believed expecting the worst helped him prepare for every situation, yet I believed expecting the worst wasted energy on negativity.

We approached life differently, but we both wanted to live for life, not death. As Kel and I flourished, our beliefs united our lives into one.

Denial was something I had lived with and survived; the reality I envisioned was something that seemed too difficult. I predicted an outcome, forfeited my power, and hid from the truth because I didn't believe in a positive outcome. When I embraced my gayness, I was able to break through walls, build a strong platform, and share an incredible life with a man named Kelly. My hospital room breakdowns reminded me of how I felt when I predicted a dismal future, so I shifted my focus and started to believe anything and everything was possible, which made others fear I was in denial. I heard all of the dismal statistics, but as long as my partner breathed, I was going to celebrate his life. Until the day one of us passed, we were one life.

## Friday, October 14, 2011

Breakfast: it was the last hospital meal, with a surprising first. Kelly grabbed his utensils, placed a piece of meat in his mouth, and while he chewed, his facial expression soured. He spit the meat back onto the plate and proclaimed, "I'm done with meat, I've gone vegan … well not entirely, but mostly." I had been encouraging Kelly to eat healthier, and we were discovering foods that tasted good also fought cancer. He was listening and hearing what his body needed. I assured everyone in the room I had nothing to do with Kelly's statement, but I was definitely elated by it.

It took time to get discharged, and we were ready way before the hospital staff. As Kel lifted himself out of bed and prepared to sit in his wheelchair, he said, "I feel good." He clung to the words as if he was surprised by how he was feeling. Waiting patiently in his chair, Kel said, "I'd rather be a Wall Fish than be in here." As always, he kept us laughing. While we waited, he looked at me and said, "This must be boring for you."

While Kel was in the hospital, many awful scenarios were discussed in front of him. When we arrived at home, I wanted a guarantee everyone would speak about Kelly as if he were awake and listening. Negativity could have its place but only outside of Kelly's earshot. This was a new beginning and very much a celebration. Kel was very capable, and I intended to surround him with energy that evoked health.

"Yay!" That was the word he uttered when I told Kel we could go home. On our way, he said, "We made it, Joey. We got through it!" I planned on wheeling him into our house, but he wanted to walk. I cried a tear or two—maybe three or four—as he made his way to the front door. It felt so great to be at home base. Everything felt possible, and we were clearly where Kel and I wanted and needed to be: at home, to live.

## Saturday, October 15, 2011

The peace and comfort of our bed felt so right that the three of us slept with little movement. Kel's body temperature remained consistent throughout the night, but he woke with some pain and wasn't shy administering an extra dose of medication. He tried to recall events from his hospital stay, and I could see the vacancy in his memory disturbed him. Filling in his blanks took a backseat to our celebratory at-home status. Showering, walking, eating, drinking ... everything felt healthier and routine. Voicing concern, Kel asked me, "Am I getting enough nutrition? I feel like I am." He was determined.

I had gone home on Thursday night to grab a change of clothes and supplies. I happened to notice our fish was sick and his aquarium needed to be cleaned. I vowed to clean it when Kel was home from the hospital. At home now and talking with my sister, I noticed our fish was lying on the rocks. I broke down, cried on her shoulder, and said, "If he sacrificed himself for Kel, I'm okay with it." We laughed through our tears, and shockingly the fish moved. We laughed louder, and I immediately removed the fish from the tainted water and cleaned his home. Kelly was the fish guy. I didn't know anything about aquariums, and I was less than thrilled with this task. With a clean aquarium, the fish was back home, but he still wasn't doing well. His tail and nose were in the rocks, and random bubbles verified he was still alive. It was a grim situation, and many of our guests counted him out. I felt I had tried everything and felt guilty I couldn't save him. Kel asked if I prepped the tank. I said, "*What?* What do you mean, prep the tank? Of course I didn't. I've never cleaned this." Kelly told me I needed to neutralize the water, so I ran and added the chemicals. I hoped and prayed, and even spoke to this little fish. He was limp and lifeless other than his gill movement when he gasped for life. The doubters remained, but I told them, "This little guy has gone through a lot. I'm not counting him out, and as long as he moves, there is hope!" Upon waking, we were informed, "The fish is alive and swimming happily." I wasn't sure when his expiration date was, but I knew I couldn't count out his own will. It was a happy moment and a miracle in its own right. Our home was about life, never counting out the possible even if things looked dark and grim. The will within decided the fate; we had to trust in it. Miracle, our fish with an enormous will, passed away May 21, 2012. I have created a children's book commemorating his life: *Miracle, My Fish Friend.*

Our home was filled from noon until early morning, and everyone emitted positive energy. Several times, I inquired if it was too much, and Kel always replied, "I am having fun. I'm having a good time." Whether he overdid it or not, the most important thing was being surrounded by love, and we embraced it. We had previous plans to attend my Dad's birthday celebration, but travel was out of the question. Kelly called my dad and told him, "We wish we could be there, Pop, but a few things came up." Kel laughed, as did everyone who heard his comment. My family was divided between my parents' home in St. Paul and our home in Duluth—one hundred-fifty miles apart—but bonded and celebrating together.

## Sunday, October 16, 2011

I had to deal with the possibility of a last hug, kiss, and good-bye—inevitable realities that were fortunately postponed. I questioned my stability. My cries were gut-wrenching and out of control but expressed my emotions deeply and fully. I was not holding back; the way I processed was purely instinctual. I was more than aware of the impact one person could have on another. I was grateful for the love Kel had awakened in me. I believed anything and everything was possible, but could I save him? Try as I might, his cure was never in my control. I was a key that unlocked some of his inhibitions, and he unlocked mine. We saved one another from loneliness and built a life of togetherness. Physically, we fought for his survival, but spiritually, we were accepting. Our days flowed with meaning and purpose. Every journey was worthwhile, and we wanted another day to live and experience more.

## Monday, October 17, 2011

Anxiety took hold, and I assumed it was caused by something I didn't do, needed to do, or should have done. My prayers were answered, I was granted my wishes, I received my requests, but what I forgot to do was be grateful. Rather than be grateful and thankful, I walked around wanting more. One look at Kel and I became grateful for the fortunes I received. We had more time to be grateful for more.

During the day, Kel's primary hospice representative stopped by. He looked at Kel and said, "Knowing how you looked on Friday and seeing you today it is an amazing transformation." He admitted every professional questioned whether discharging Kel was the right thing to do. He acknowledged it was. Kel had good coloring; he was determined and willing to tackle projects. It was a magnificent improvement.

## Tuesday, October 18, 2011

Pain control was under adjustment. Sleep was a privilege that had been lost. I was administering medication throughout the night and working around the house during the day. I may have been burning the candle at both ends, but I wasn't burning out. Many people felt a miracle had already occurred: Kel's homecoming. When he took his time and rested as needed, Kel was able to accomplish many things. Per his decision, we shopped, and he walked quite far. I was proud of his progress and hoped he was too. When he declared his vegan status, his eating habits followed, and I was a full supporter, encourager, and participant. We did it together and reaped the benefits. There was always knowledge to attain, and Kel and I gained life through health choices. We embraced who we were, decided what we wanted, made the changes, and believed everything was working.

## Wednesday, October 19, 2011

Early in the morning, Kel was admitted into the hospital. His pain and digestive system were out of whack. The pain medication had affected Kel's regularity, and aids had been taken orally to counteract potential binding problems. Over the course of nine months, Kelly had regularly dealt with constipation and discovered ways to combat it. Unfortunately, his successful tactics were attempted too late in this circumstance. X-rays proved what we had already known: he was bloated and full. This condition increased pain and created a whole new issue. Hospice staff planned on monitoring his pain level (and tweaking accordingly) once things were functioning normally. We planned to flush these issues along with the rest of the shit!

Progress was ridiculously slow, and Kelly's discomfort was very apparent. This was the first time I heard him question "Why?" His eyes were sad and tear-filled when he asked, "What is taking so long?" Kelly's excruciating pains were caused by constipation, not cancer, but still his pain medications were increased to astronomical levels. Though I shared the extreme measures Kel had previously taken at home when dealing with this issue, I didn't feel heard, and the proceedings were unchanged. They continued to treat him for pains that they believed were caused by his cancer. Kel's cancer pain was always in his chest and upper back, but when they asked where his pains were, Kel pointed to his stomach. I restated what I had said so many other times: "He is constipated! That is what is causing him pain." The doctor proceeded at his educated pace. Kel managed to sleep for a short time but was still lacking relief and comfort. As Kel drifted in and out, he was making several football references. Was he kidding? He asked me if a game was on and then said, "Second down, fourth quarter." He made another comment about the Vikings, and I knew we had a serious problem. Not only were we dealing with constipation, but Kelly was showing signs of an alter-ego. He needed sleep.

## Thursday, October 20, 2011

Approximately thirty-six hours later, Kel finally received some relief, but he was now under the control of an extreme dose of painkillers that had zero effect on the pain he was experiencing from constipation. The reason he was admitted was to gain relief: he was in need of a BM. Kel wondered why it was taking so long, and his eyes cried for relief. What could I have done differently?

For the first time, I too found myself asking why. Since his diagnosis, I was by Kel's side as much as possible, and I gained knowledge, experience, and insight. I saw how he was affected mentally and physically; I charted what I saw and assisted him in every way I could. I was aware of the cycles he'd go through, the changes that took effect when medications were changed or altered, the signs when he was heading down the road of sleep-deprivation, and the consequences of sleepless nights.

I knew his abilities, and we discovered more capabilities. I learned how to encourage foods and supplements so they were accepted. I absolutely knew when he was at the end of his rope. He shared enough information with me that I could recognize issues by sight while he was dealing with them physically. His breathing patterns fluctuated, and I could tell if he was having a dream or nightmare or if there was a serious problem. I knew his calorie intake, his personal regimen, how much water he drank. I learned so much about Kel I would question him on his questionnaires regarding his pain levels, quality of life, etc., because I knew if his answers reflected his current status. We shared our wishes regarding life and death. I was the cause of arguments as I tried to gain perspective and understanding in an effort to better assist him. Why did I do all of this? Because I loved him! Trying to help Kelly gave me purpose during a crucial time, and I was going to keep on looking, learning, searching, hoping, wishing, praying, and believing.

I was frustrated by hindsight, regret, feeling unheard, and a lack of communication. I sifted through circumstances that could have and should have gone differently, acknowledging my role as Kelly's advocate. It was my responsibility to ask and ask again, to tell and tell again, to share my thoughts and opinions, because I knew Kel like no other. I may have lacked a degree in medicine, but I was well-versed and educated in Kelly Boedigheimer. Next time, they would hear me and listen to what I had to say.

Kelly slept better than he had in three days, but not before I had to remind staff to administer the drug that helped him relax. Sleep, internal plumbing system, and pain control—keeping them balanced made Kelly a happy guy.

## Friday, October 21, 2011

I felt as if I had been speaking into deaf ears, and I was ready to pull them off and scream into them as they lay in the palm of my hand. What part of Kelly's history wasn't understood? I had been told, "Rest assured, we all want the same thing. You can trust us. He's in good hands." What Kelly received was their failure to accept the knowledge available to them from an outside source. They heard, "Pain," and treated that to the best of their ability, even if it meant knocking him unconscious. Pain was treated first, regardless of the underlying condition, which happened to be constipation. I was communicating my concerns, but apparently their receiver was turned off.

I had two separate conversations, and I knew I'd be heard. During my first conversation, I was told, "We try to make sure that our patients are at a pain level of zero."

I responded, "Are you aware Kel told hospice, on the day he was admitted, his pain level goal was three? He wanted to be alert and awake, not knocked out and unconscious." Kelly's file was immediately changed to reflect his original wishes.

The second conversation began with this statement: "I feel we did everything correctly in treating Kelly, and I would do it all over the exact same way."

To which I asked, "Even after I shared his history and explained the extremes we had to take at home, you would still say you did the right thing? If I had been a bit more obstinate and verbal, do you think you would have moved a little faster?"

He said, "Possibly."

It was difficult being around people who were preparing for my loved one's demise. Going home had never felt so right. For us, as long as Kel lived and breathed, hope remained within. Kelly's light was still shining bright; it was a beacon attracting every ounce of positive energy and uniting it with his life force.

In our own bed, there was a peace that came over all of us—the safe comfort of togetherness. We all drifted to different dream locations, but we stayed connected throughout the night. Our dreams reminded us anything and everything was possible.

## Saturday, October 22, 2011

Everything was better at home. Kel was becoming more aware and alert while nutritional and household routines were getting back on track. Kelly's family hadn't recently visited, so we drove there and surprised them. I shared how I caught Kel walking around our house attempting small tasks, which we finished together. He was determined, brave, and willing to be as independent as possible. I was proud of him, and he heard those words from my lips, over and over.

As we headed home, I asked Kelly if there was any place he wanted to go. He told me yes, but in my mind I questioned if he really needed to because it would require a bit of walking. I stopped, and we walked through the store. Kelly wanted to check out the Halloween items, and through his tear-filled eyes, he said, "I know we don't need any more decorations but I am buying these because it makes me believe I will be here to celebrate." I treasured his positive perspective and extended my hope.

Impressed was an understatement. I was amazed, happy, overwhelmed, and ecstatic at his day's accomplishments. It reminded me to never assume Kelly had limitations because he was continually proving his capabilities.

## Sunday, October 23, 2011.

After the past months, I still found myself getting settled and comfortable. The only way to approach life was day by day—actually, moment by moment. I was floating on a cloud as Kel's momentum lifted my spirits, and then suddenly his pain spiked. He tried position after position, but nothing eased his pain, and the circumstance was dismal at best. Our spirits were broken with every attempt to gain comfort. It was gut-wrenching. When a cozy position was found, it lasted only moments before the piercing pain took over. This situation was anything but new, except this time we were able to take a different approach. Kelly's PICC came with twenty-four-hour support, and through a step-by-step process, I was able to adjust his pain medication. For a few hours, he gained some peace and comfort.

Pain remained Kel's biggest fear, and witnessing him in pain left me feeling useless, but we made major strides as we relied on each other until we gained some relief.

## Monday, October 24, 2011.

It was a beautiful day to absorb what life had to offer. Kelly stepped out our front door and commented on how good the fresh air felt as it reached his lungs. His eyes looked to the sky as he inhaled, embracing every breath. After making his way to my car, he sobbed and told me, "I feel like this could be my last nice day. I'm afraid I only have a couple days left." There weren't any rose-colored glasses rosy enough to help me see a prettier picture, and I wanted to deny his words. I was crushed from the weight of his emotions but I tried to offer whatever comfort I could. We hadn't planned on seeing his parents, but I knew he needed their love and support. He slept much of the drive, and when we arrived at his folks' house, I pulled his wheelchair from the trunk. I asked Kelly if he told them he had become reliant on the chair. He hadn't. His mom and dad came outdoors, greeted us with hugs, and suggested we take a walk. Kel used his chair for support and we headed toward the end of the block. Tears ran down his face, so I grabbed him, hugged him, and, through my tears, I told him I was proud. Every step was a struggle but I knew Kel had a personal goal within, and he intended to reach it. When he got to the end of the block, I helped him into his chair and pushed him the remainder of the way. I was so amazed by Kelly, I fell in love with him, but he was so much more than I ever realized.

We faced extremely difficult moments and took turns lifting the other up when needed. If I was down, he would pick me up, and vice-versa. Before we left our home, we made a toast using freshly squeezed juice. It didn't matter what the toast was because we were fortunate and grateful to have had another day together, sharing moments created through unexpected circumstances. In the evening, at home, we sat together and acknowledged the day wasn't less than perfect—it was better than!

# Chapter Eleven

## When He's Ready

### Wednesday, October 26, 2011

I could no longer look at Kel and distinguish his pain level—it had become constant. As pain continuously beat on him, I think it became harder for him to decipher what level it was. Attempts to increase medication had become futile, and his fear of pain had succumbed to acceptance. The previous forty-eight hours consisted of several conversations leading us to this day. We had fought side by side, encouraging, supporting, and loving each other, striving for comfort and peace. We had thirteen and a half amazing, wonderful years together—forever united but soon to part. Kelly told me he was ready.

We both wanted Kelly to spend the remainder of life at home, but he held several reasons for choosing to live them out in hospice: he wanted to lift the burden upon me. I hated his decision, and I sought every possible option for a different outcome. This was Kel's wish, a change from what we had agreed upon, but I had to accept it. I questioned my own ability to follow him to the hospital because I wasn't sure if I'd be able to handle being in that place again.

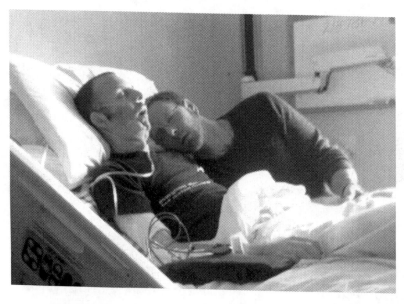

Hours after he was admitted, family surrounded Kel's bedside. His pain was horrific, and breathing was difficult. I held him close in attempts to comfort both of us. We were afraid this was our journey's end. Tears filled the room, and moments passed. Kel was saying his final good-byes. To his parents, he said, "You two need to stay together and quit fighting and stop bickering so much. Show more love; start showing that you love each other like you have shown me love during these past weeks. Everybody needs to stay strong and go after what you love. If you love it … go for it!" Silence came over everyone but was broken when Kel told me had to pee. After I cleared the room, Kel said, "I thought I was going to die … and then I didn't." It wasn't the words that touched me, it was the way he spoke them: "I thought I was going to die" was spoken with fear and disbelief. "And then I didn't" was said with amazement while fluctuating to a question. We celebrated with tears and laughter.

His pain was under the best control ever; unfortunately, that meant a dream state. I had the privilege of spending the entire evening by Kel's side. As the hours passed, I fell in and out of consciousness. Heartache struck me every waking moment, and tears flowed with little control. I whispered in Kel's ear (probably annoying the shit out of him as he tried to sleep), going through a checklist of things I thought could be weighing on his mind. I was still trying to do everything and anything to help ease any heaviness he had.

## Thursday, October 27, 2011

Our once envisioned future had been drastically altered, and I needed to trust and believe that wonderful things were still possible. I know he sensed my fear and pain, and I sensed his. Though Kel was unable to eat or drink, he wasn't ready to leave us; he just wanted the pain to go away. Unfortunately, one was not attainable without the other. His physical and mental awareness was a gift, allowing us time to share our love, kisses, hugs, and words of encouragement. I had typically yearned for more, but I took comfort in what could have been our last face-to-face conscious encounter. Oh, the hurt I felt. I said to Kel, "My grieving wouldn't be so hard if you weren't such an awesome person to celebrate." After all, I was celebrating what we had shared. I was unprepared for its lack of continuation, but both of us had to continue on our path.

My emotions peaked and flowed, flushing my fear and pain away so the celebration of life could emerge—a celebration of Kel's life. We had much to celebrate, and I refused to question the grand scheme, even though it sucked. Kel's journey continued, and I embraced the fortunes he brought me. I was so proud of my guy. Thirteen-plus years earlier, we found each other and lived.

## Friday, October 28, 2011

Kel became restless and removed his oxygen mask. I struggled to decipher his needs. Throughout the night, there were moments I believed he would join our fallen loved ones. Around 3:00 a.m., he lay in his bed, and I told Kelly, "He is waiting for you with open arms." Kelly acknowledged with a grunting sound. I asked, "Are you going to keep Him waiting?"

Intentionally and clearly, Kel sounded, "Uh-huh!" Just like a gay, Kelly was taking his time and the party would have to wait for him. Around 5:00 a.m., we found comfort and sleep.

In the morning, he was more alert, and I could tell he wanted to open his eyes. I wiped them clean, and he flashed his beautiful green eyes. They roamed the room swiftly and briefly to absorb his surroundings. Twice, he mumbled to me, "I love you," as he pursed his lips to give me a kiss. It was a gift I had only dreamed. He even asked for me because he wanted to let me know he was experiencing some pain. His coloring was a bit better, and he made it clear he did not want the oxygen back on. For much of the day, we absorbed the laughs while our tears sat in waiting.

While Kel was on this journey, I was on my own, unaware of how it would play out. Time had very few rules, and Kelly seemed to be ruling time. With all of our blessings, he could free himself. He held on, but for what? Every moment was a blessing, and every minute was a healing opportunity to process the truth of life's reality.

## Saturday, October 29, 2011

I wanted a miracle, and life was full of them. The day I met Kel was a miracle I'd discover years later. As the days passed, I realized how much Kel loved having people surround him. He was relaxed when people were near, and he slept soundly as we cuddled in his single hospital bed. Hospice staff welcomed our overflowing love and support system, which made Kelly's hospital stay an incredibly rich experience.

A Halloween party planned for our home was moved to Kelly's room. It had always been his favorite holiday. Several of us wondered, "Was he waiting for this?" Kel's room was filled with family and friends celebrating the Halloween season. Laughter and descriptions coincided as Kel's ears painted the images for his mind. He was very aware of his surroundings, and he opened his eyes long enough to see what his ears had been hearing. He smiled as he embraced his family of loved ones. My sister asked, "Kel, are you enjoying the Halloween party?"

With open eyes and a grin, he said, "Yep, it's in my honor!"

I whispered in Kel's ear, "I love you," and as he started to say it back, a hiccup stopped him at, "*I lo,*" and he never finished his sentence. I asked him if there was more he wanted to say, and he scrunched his face as if he had something really important to share. We quickly quieted every noise source. With thought and focus, Kelly forcefully stated, "My feet!" Kel's feet became extremely sensitive after chemo, and his sister was sprawled over them (not on them) at the end of his bed; the sheets had constricted and added pressure. Kelly's profound statement ended the quietness and generated a riotous moment. He drifted back to sleep while the love and laughter continued to blanket him.

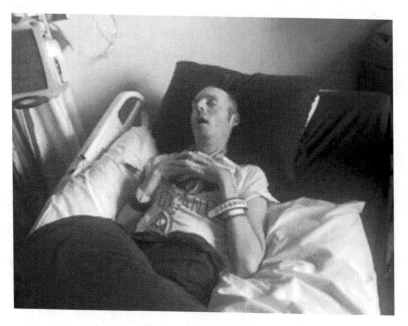

## Sunday, October 30, 2011

I slept alongside Kelly until 10:45 a.m. The bed wasn't comfortable but it definitely was comforting. I'd like to say I felt refreshed, but my heart was heavy and my mind remained aware of the circumstances. He slept much of the day and had very few interactions, but in the morning, he did say, "It's very quiet." The party continued throughout the day. Kel's room revolved with people bringing their love and laughter. At bedtime, *The Golden Girls*, one of Kel's favorite sitcoms, graced the TV. I hoped their sweet, funny, comedic delivery would bring forth happy memories—light-hearted material drowning out sadness, fears, and worries. I was grateful Kel was my partner, and I thanked him for being my friend.

Any reason why Kelly's life had to be taken paled in comparison as to why I needed him. My life became better when he was by my side, and having to walk alone was a very scary thought. I found it surreal that life would continue. I found it difficult to imagine happiness without him near. My heart and soul felt as if they were being torn from my body, but I knew that would cease when I was able to heal as I learned to accept. I was functioning at a stable level, but there were times I felt like my legs would buckle as the weight of sadness buried me. How long could I rely on others to be near me 24/7, to guide me through difficult times and talk me through my tears? At some point, I knew I'd have to stand on my own, live alone, make my meals, and complete all the daily chores that a home requires. Many people do and function normally, but it would be my first attempt in a world that was unfamiliar and appeared lonely. I also knew healing had begun because my appreciation, gratitude, and sense of opportunity made appearances. They may have been brief, but they were there.

## Monday, October 31, 2011

Last night, it was difficult to understand Kel, but I heard his sentence. Hoping I was wrong, I whispered his words into his ear and followed them with "Did I hear you correctly?" I knew he was preparing me when he said, "Tonight is my last night." When we woke, Kel's declining health was apparent, but believing his suffering could soon be over brought peace.

Kel's favorite holiday had arrived: Halloween. There was a knock on his hospital door, and a cute little lady asked if we would like to hear some harp music. The moment she strummed the strings, I was affected. I put my computer aside and joined Kel on his bed. There was something angelic and peaceful in the sound, and I knew it was resonating through Kel. Tears fell from my eyes and made their way onto Kel as I embraced him. "Amazing Grace" was her final piece, and my emotions were taken on a journey I hadn't packed for. It would be the last song Kel and I would physically share together.

Before going home to shower and change, I whispered to Kelly, "I hope you will wait for me, but I understand if you have to go. I love you so much."

"Tonight is my last night" replayed in my head as I attempted to make myself look attractive for Kel. Upon my return, Kelly was in distress. Anger was my first reaction, as I found Kel's suffering inhumane. I took his side and loved him.

As we held hands, unconditional love flowed between us. Kelly's peace was my only desire, even though the world as I knew it would no longer exist. My love replaced every fear as I encouraged him to leave his pain and suffering behind. Reminding him of my blind faith, I wanted him to trust the unknown. I assured him I would be good, and quickly restated, "No, I'll be great! You can go, Kel. Give it a chance. If you don't like what you see, turn around and come back to me.

I'll be right here waiting." With his one-way ticket to freedom, Kelly arrived safely. No longer within our limitations, he was illuminated.

I lived the next hour unselfishly and unconditionally celebrating Kelly's spirit. My future without him was upon me, but elation showered my soul. My smile was wide, and I was proud as peace filled me from head to toe. My internal light was shining bright, honoring the life and love of Kelly. Awareness was gained throughout this journey of living, and I would move forward in a positive light.

*Forever in my heart and soul. I love you, Buck-A-Roo!*

## Kelly's Obituary

Kelly "Kel" Michael Boedigheimer, 39, of Duluth, made Heaven his home on Monday, Oct. 31, 2011, after losing a nine-month battle to Melanoma. He was born in Cloquet on Dec. 17, 1971, to Francis and Joan (McKibbon) Boedigheimer.

His partner and best friend, Joe Peterson, was at his side for more than 13 years while they built a life together based on love and commitment. He loved to travel, host parties and spend time with their best buddy, Chaos. Kel loved having people around him and was surrounded by many that loved him deeply. The prayers for a miracle to extend his life were not meant to be, but everyone who knew him came to realize that the true miracle was he came into their lives and thus will live forever. His sense of humor and quick wit would illuminate a room and he continued to entertain until the end. His spirit surrounds his loved ones and they will always remember his smile, which fills them with peace.

Kelly worked for Black Bear Casino for nearly 20 years and formed multiple, lasting friendships with the staff and coworkers. He was well-respected as an honest, fair and considerate employee and manager. He loved his job and his Black Bear family.

Kelly will be missed by everyone that knew him, especially Joe who loved him like no other; his parents; sisters Cindy (George) Meger, and Tammy (Larry) Zeadow; brother, Scott; seven nieces including Marisa, Lindsay, Alycia, Jennifer, Rebekka, Carroline, Sammantha; and one nephew, Cody. He will be dearly missed by his many wonderful friends and large extended family, the

Petersons, who loved and welcomed him as a son, brother and uncle.

Joe and the family wish to thank the Hospice staff at Essentia for their compassionate care and concern during the past month. There will be a CELEBRATION OF LOVE TO HONOR THIS AMAZING MAN.

**The memorial stone is located at Sunrise Memorial in Hermantown, Minnesota—a tranquil location was sought. Kel's remains, along with cards, letters, and special memorabilia he had given me, are placed within.**

Joe Peterson

# The Celebration of Kel's Life

Days before his passing, celebration arrangements were discussed. Kel's silence was his approval, and it was time to take action. I planned to honor Kelly and the life we shared with a celebration much like a wedding reception we should have been able to have.

With help from four friends, we gathered at my home to create photo boards for Kel's celebration. As we reminisced, the tear fairy struck. While looking at photographs from 2011, I realized how visually unaware I was during Kelly's transformational journey. It was late evening when two friends decided to leave, and I thought, *Good, I can chill for a little bit and let Kel entertain the other two.* This was an unexpected slip of my reality but a testament to how Kel and I leaned on one another. The vacancy in my life was felt, and I needed to find the footing he once helped balance.

My mind accepted Kel had moved on, but my heart and soul had trouble adjusting. Much of the past nine months had revolved around Kelly's health, and while I planned his celebration, I was still living and breathing for him. Even with the same results, I would have done it over because I experienced a greater purpose and meaning in my life. Regardless if I could have done things differently and possibly better, Kel lived life his way: whole-heartedly and positively. He may have been afraid, but he was never angry over his circumstances.

Much like his internal light, the celebration of Kel's life shined bright. On November 12, positive energy radiated from hundreds of loved ones, united as we honored Kelly. Thank you, Kel—you lived vibrantly and brilliantly. I love you.

## Sunday, November 13, 2011

During the summer of 2011, Kelly received a care package from the family of a former female classmate. Inside was a hope bracelet made by her daughter. Kelly wore it faithfully and had it on when he was cremated. The day after the celebration, I met this classmate's family. It was an unplanned visit, and her daughter handed me a drawing addressed "To: Joe." Before I looked at it, she said, "I made this last night, and I didn't know what I was going to do with it."

The picture made me teary-eyed, and I asked, "Did you know what the theme of the celebration was?" Of course she didn't; no one knew, and her mom was already at the celebration when she was creating the drawing. I turned the picture around so the family could see it. Then I said, "The theme was rainbows." She had drawn a rainbow with one flower below its colorful arch.

Unexplainable, beautiful things were happening around me while I planned the celebration. I felt Kelly's presence and believed he was assisting me. For the celebration, rainbow arches were formed using tables, and tablecloths brought their colors to life. At a gold table at the end of the rainbow sat our parents and me; Kelly's urn was the centerpiece. Kelly was every color of the rainbow, representing the togetherness of sun and rain, yin and yang.

# Epilogue: Closure

I believed it was possible to save Kelly's life, and when I failed, undeserved guilt consumed me. Finding restitution required admitting my abilities while releasing my unrealistic capabilities. Unsettling questions and professional judgment errors prompted me to reconnect with previous caregivers. During several conversations, their apologies were extended as their awareness was heightened, hopefully resulting in better patient care. Regardless of the communicative outcome, I needed to be heard and release the burdens that plagued my psyche. After every discussion, I shined a little brighter. Love may not have been a cure but it certainly made life worth living.

Kelly and I could have faced cancer with fear and denial, but too much of our lives had already been lived that way. We battled our bullies and haters, but the worst offenders were within. I despised myself for being something other than what I thought was acceptable by societal standards. Suicidal thoughts ran rampant as I sought freedom from this painful world. Try as I might, I couldn't change my attraction toward men. Recently, I became aware of the correlation between my gay struggles and Kelly's survival. My thinking, *Nothing I do is good enough*, was a result of unsuccessfully attaining heterosexual status. Six months after Kelly's death, I became aware *Nothing I do is good enough* had become my life's credo and a continued source of my guilt. I now know my future is unforeseen, yet every aspect of it will contain my entire history. The only way I can leave my weighted world behind is through acceptance.

In late summer 2011, I informed Kelly I was in talks with a publisher, and the conversation segued into discussing our goals and aspirations. Reflecting upon my own, I asked Kel to share his childhood dreams. He said he never had any. I was dumbfounded and said, "Really, you never had any? That seems so sad." I just couldn't imagine my life without dreams. As I replayed our conversation, I began to envy Kelly. He didn't need to dream because he was living one. Whatever Kel wanted, he lived. Upon sharing our final chapter together, writing became my dream. Kelly no longer stands by my side, but his spirit is within, guiding me. No matter how lonely and painful my life after his death had become, there were awesome things happening all around me. When I accepted that, I was awakened to the beauty that blossomed and flourished everywhere. Life may not have worked out the way I envisioned, but it's working out the way it is supposed to.

After living life the way Kel and I did, I refused to crumble under the reality of what was. We lived and lived well, and I am alive. My happiness and success will honor the life we shared and the unity that was us. Moments before Kelly left my world, I whispered in his ear and made a vow: "I'll be fine, Kel. I'll be good. Scratch that. I'll be *great!* I promise."

*If you love it … go for it!*

# Our Thanks

Black Bear Casino went above and beyond in supporting us throughout the journey. They were a generous contributor for the benefit and the celebration of Kel's life. The Black Bear members, staff, and employees contributed gifts, dollars, and vacation hours to express their love and show their support for a valued member of their family. When Kel could no longer continue working, Black Bear threw him a retirement celebration. The casino members honored Kelly's twenty years of devoted service and guaranteed he'd have a place to call home.

The Kraft team also went above and beyond. Their support allowed me to physically and mentally be where I was needed. They too contributed to the benefit and continually supported me regardless of scheduling conflicts or appointments. Kel often wondered if my position was in danger, and my supervisors always assured my employment was secure. Kel and I were both very fortunate.

The Benefit Gang threw an event that made Kelly feel like a celebrity. The initiative of these special people gave Kel a once-in-a-lifetime opportunity to bask in the love of so many. These individuals communicated with businesses near and far, and successfully attained donations while raising support for Kelly's care. Together, they increased melanoma awareness and increased the positive energy within our world.

Several individuals and couples blessed us with care packages, gifts, and meals. Each and every one was given and received with *love!* As the course of action changed, so did the gifts put forth. All of us were striving for a miraculous outcome. Many times, Kel and I would cry over the generosity and love that would greet us every day. Kelly often felt unworthy, but he was always grateful.

Family: our families united and bonded with each other long before Kel's diagnosis, and they continued to be a driving force during this journey. Kel and I were accepted into each other's families as if we were legally recognized as a member. We were welcomed as family, and each of us was loved like a son, brother-in-law, and uncle. This fortune of acceptance only added to the loving riches we already attained from each other. We were able to live freely within the company of family, the most precious gift for us. I must specifically thank my sister, Sue, because she listened and guided me daily while being burdened with the weight of my world. It wasn't hers to carry, but she did it for Kel and me, and we were blessed and grateful. Thank you: Sue, Diane and Cassie for reading my prepublished words and sharing your insights!

Friends: people who were there to love us even when you despised us. The spectrums of friendship are vast, but we felt your individual love and support, and sometimes we questioned our worthiness. So many wonderful memories, events, outings, and celebrations were created for us through your acts of kindness and visions of brightness. If there is a string of words that could express our physical, emotional, and mental gratitude, I am unable to find the correct combination to do it justice. Friends are the family we've chosen. Thank you for choosing us.

Caring Bridge: our written journey began with you. The unity of spirits, energies, hopes, beliefs, and prayers were made possible through CB. It was the internet at its very best. A caring bridge, which we crossed together, was created between resources and willing participants. There were many individuals and institutions that also felt like caring bridges: The VFW in Carlton, Private Party Donators, Rock-A-Billy Revue, Elvis aka Ken Sutherland, the drag show committee and performers, the Flame Nightclub, the Mayo Clinic in Rochester, Essentia Health in Duluth, St. Mary's Hospice in Duluth, Cremation Society of Minnesota, Memorial Donators, Sunrise Memorial Park in Duluth, North Country Dental, stylists Julie Dahl and Alex Jost, Pawsh Grooming and Crow-Goebel Veterinary Clinic.

Kelly "Kel" Boedigheimer: thank you for sharing over thirteen years of personal growth, greatness, and warmth. Our relationship was a door into a world that I only thought I'd view from a window.

**Faces: the face of Life and the face of Words.**